Parents on Dyslexia

Multilingual Matters

Bilingual Children: From Birth to Teens
  GEORGE SAUNDERS
Bilingualism: Basic Principles
  HUGO BAETENS BEARDSMORE
Child Language Disability: Implications in an Educational Setting
  KAY MOGFORD and JANE SADLER (eds)
ESL: A Handbook for Teachers and Administrators in International Schools
  EDNA MURPHY (ed.)
The Path to Language
  DANIELLE BOUVET
Language Acquisition: The Age Factor
  D. M. SINGLETON
Oral Language Across the Curriculum
  DAVID CORSON
Raising Children Bilingually: The Pre-School Years
  LENORE ARNBERG
Sign and School
  JIM KYLE (ed.)
Story as Vehicle
  EDIE GARVIE

Please contact us for the latest book information:
Multilingual Matters,
Bank House, 8a Hill Road,
Clevedon, Avon BS21 7HH,
England.

Parents on Dyslexia

Edited by Saskia van der Stoel

Translated by G. D. Burton

MULTILINGUAL MATTERS LTD
Clevedon • Philadelphia

Library of Congress Cataloging in Publication Data

Ouders over Dyslexie. English.
Parents on Dyslexia/Edited by Saskia van der Stoel;
Translated by G. D. Burton.
p. cm.
Translation of: Ouders over Dyslexie
1 Dyslexic children — Family relationships.
2. Parent and child.
I. Stoel, Saskia van der. II. Title.
RJ496.A509313   1990
618.92′8553 — dc20

British Library Cataloguing in Publication Data

van der Stoel, Saskia.
Parents on Dyslexia.
1. Children. Dyslexia.
I. Title. II. Ouders over Dyslexie. English.
618.928553

ISBN 1-85359-077-0
ISBN 1-85359-076-2 (pbk)

Multilingual Matters Ltd

Bank House, 8a Hill Road,   &   1900 Frost Road, Suite 101,
Clevedon, Avon BS21 7HH,   Bristol, PA 19007,
England.   USA.

Copyright © 1990 Saskia van der Stoel
Translated by G. D. Burton

First published in 1987 under the title *Ouders over Dyslexie* by
Lemniscaat b.v., Rotterdam, The Netherlands.

Typeset by Editorial Enterprises, Torquay, Devon.
Printed and bound in Great Britain by Billing & Sons Ltd.

Contents

Preface

Dyslexia is often a controversial subject in educational circles the world over. It is equally so in Britain. There is no definition that is generally acceptable to all educationalists. It is most frequently used to describe children who fail to learn to read in spite of intact senses, adequate teaching and normal emotional development. It may be that it is associated with specific neurological malfunctioning or malformation. There is no hard evidence either way. The research that has been carried out is conflicting and ambiguous. There seems to be a tendency for researchers in this particular field to fall into one camp or another.

If children are to keep pace with their general education, they need to read. Poor readers fall behind. Instead of concentrating on the contents of lessons they spend their time working out the mechanics of reading, spelling and writing. Most poor readers feel unhappy, begin to be ashamed of themselves and feel that they must be stupid as everyone around them seems to read effortlessly. The effects are not only educational but social as self-confidence and self-esteem are damaged.

The skills involved in learning to read are complex. Talking, an understanding of words, the recognition of shapes and the blending of sounds are a few of the skills needed before reading can begin. Some children after only a year or two's schooling have experienced continual failure. Pressure from peers and adults does not help.

Are these children dyslexic? Is it helpful to use the term? One of the arguments against its use is that it suggests a condition which will be there for life. Yet many children who fail to progress with reading are eventually taught to overcome their problems successfully. There are many indicators that children may have difficulties in learning to read or write. Some children who are left-handed seem to find reading more difficult than those who are right-handed. However, the vast majority of left-handed children learn to read as quickly as everyone else.

Another argument against its use is that it can lower motivation — 'I'm dyslexic, I can't read' — or that it lowers expectations — 'He's dyslexic, he won't be able to cope with that'.

These arguments can be turned round of course. There are many children who, finding that they are dyslexic, no longer feel failures — their confidence and self-esteem grows. 'I'm not stupid, I'm dyslexic and so reading is difficult, just like some children who cannot run fast — nobody says they are stupid for not running!'

Similarly as long as we are searching and researching for evidence as to the causes of reading difficulties we may come up with at least a partial answer. There is some evidence of neurological misfunctions in adults who acquire reading difficulties after illness or accidents.

Many local education authorities and educational psychologists prefer to use the term 'specific learning difficulty' rather than dyslexia. However there are just as many arguments against this term. If it is 'specific', what is the answer? — that too should be specific. All too often the difficulty cannot be pin-pointed. All too often seemingly appropriate remedial measures have no effect.

Those of us who have spent some time working with children who are learning to read have come across children who (for no apparent reason) fail to learn. Their writing is full of inconsistencies; one word is read correctly, a similar one proves difficult and so on. If using the term dyslexia seems helpful, then use it.

The important thing is to develop the child's self-esteem. Enable him or her to relax. Children need to be valued for what they can do and sympathetically encouraged to develop strategies to cope with their difficulties in reading.

These accounts, by parents and by dyslexics themselves, give some insight into the problems and will help some parents and educationalists to avoid the pitfalls and negative happenings described here. Parents, if you are concerned, look for

sympathetic help — don't be fobbed off. Find someone whom
you can trust to help you. Educationalists, remember there is
more than one way to the truth, learning processes are varied
and variable — there is no *one* way to success. When the
debate about dyslexia rages I am always reminded of a psychologist who referred to it as ARBAON ... A rose by any other
name.

Bev McCracken
Head of Special Education
Avon Education Services

Translator's note

Although the topics covered in this book are of universal relevance, the case
histories that form its backbone are those of Dutch residents. For the transla-
tor this causes a few problems when specific examples from the Dutch educational system are mentioned. Although the overall structure of the educational
system is similar to that of many other countries, there are inevitable differences of detail. For ease of reading, the nearest English equivalent has been
used in as many places as possible, but in some cases it was felt that this
would be either misleading or too cumbersome to spell out fully each time. In
such cases the original Dutch term, or a literal translation of it, has been left
in the text, and a Glossary of these terms has been provided at the end of the
book. The first occurrence of each of these terms has been indicated by an
asterisk in the text.

Foreword

Dyslexia as it is Experienced

Dyslexia is a hidden handicap in two respects. It is a hidden handicap in the first place because it is an unknown handicap. Even children, young people and adults who are actually dyslexic scarcely know what it is, if they know at all. They experience it as an incomprehensible inability to read quickly and fluently and as a childish inability to remember exactly how words ought to be written down. It is almost always a shock when the parents of a dyslexic child discover that their son or daughter, who until then has developed so normally, is getting bogged down and is encountering problems right from the start of his or her schooldays. It is as well to realise that a learning problem like dyslexia always creates great concern for the child's future and brings about far-reaching changes in the lives of the parents and the child. The parents experience a second shock when they become aware that their child's teacher does not see the problem, does not want to see it, will not acknowledge it and simply dismisses it. In spite of the goodwill and the insight of some teachers, there are unfortunately still very many in both primary and secondary education who are in the dark regarding learning problems such as dyslexia. The parents then find themselves at the beginning of a long road, fighting a lack of understanding and striving for better, specifically directed help for their child. The parents' stories in this book are witness to this. This recognition will, I hope, give heart to all the other parents of dyslexic children.

Dyslexia is also a hidden handicap in another way. It is a handicap which people prefer to keep hidden and camouflaged by as far as possible avoiding reading and writing in their daily life. For the young person or adult who is dyslexic, dyslexia is something one is ashamed of, especially towards strangers, because they recognise only too well the prejudices in our society. The fear of being regarded as stupid, the fear of being thought inferior, the fear of not being accepted by others — this can dominate the life of a dyslexic person. For many it is an arduous and long struggle to regain their self-respect and to move in society without fear. Here too the parents' narratives in this book have a clear message.

The purpose of this book is to give the parents of dyslexic children and dyslexic people themselves the support of recognition and the courage to carry on. Its purpose is also to stimulate teachers in our educational system to reflect on the problem of dyslexia and to induce them to deepen their knowledge of it, for sooner or later they will all have to cope with it.

The book also aims to show that timely help from specialists can bring about considerable improvement and save the dyslexic child much suffering. If there is one person to whom this book ought to be dedicated, it is the mother of the dyslexic child: a token of respect for those who never cease to stand up for their children, who never give up and continue to seek the right help, convinced that, though their children do indeed have a handicap, with the right help considerable improvement can be effected and that their children's future need not be inferior to that of others.

Professor J.J. Dumont
Chairman, Dyslexia Foundation

Introduction

Dyslexia — Word Blindness — Reading Blindness — Dysgraphia — Reading and Spelling Problems... All words. Labels which can be put on the subject of this book. One word may be more suitable than another, but a single word can never be sufficient to describe such a complex phenomenon as dyslexia. Many more words are needed to do that. A whole book. And when one has finished that, perhaps other books too, as sometimes books create more questions than they can answer. I hope that this is the case with this book too. It does not pretend to be an exhaustive treatment of the concept of dyslexia, leaving the reader with the satisfied feeling that he or she now knows everything that is known about the phenomenon.

It is not the aim of this book to transfer knowledge in the form of dry, loosely connected facts. We desire primarily to cultivate an understanding of dyslexia and all that is connected with it. Secondly we aim to facilitate amongst parents of dyslexic children a form of recognition of the type: 'These are problems which my child is also having to struggle with', or 'That difficult period is behind us now'. And finally, offering a way forward, offering possible solutions, is also an important motive for writing this book.

Of course, a great deal of unconscious knowledge lies hidden in the objectives of 'understanding' and 'recognition'. They have to do with the nature of dyslexia and by definition are vague and difficult to describe. We have attempted to put them into words via those most directly involved, namely dyslexic children and their parents. There is also a contribution from an adult who is dyslexic. These descriptions of people's experiences form the principal part of the book. Each chapter contains one or more of these narratives, each of which relates to a particular question. The question is elaborated in detail in the introduction to each chapter.

Where an instinctive picture begins to emerge from the experiences of dyslexic children and their parents of what dyslexia actually is and what it means to be dyslexic, we need to be well aware that this picture is not rigidly demarcated. The child in each narrative is not a 'standard' dyslexic child. Of course, each child has characteristics which you could label dyslexic, but there is also a great deal more. He or she also has a large number of characteristics which in themselves do not have all that much to do with dyslexia. But in the course of his or her life these other characteristics, in combination with the dyslexic features, can form a specific pattern. And hence one can often no longer deduce from an experiential narrative what is typical of dyslexia and what can be put down to the child's personality or to chance circumstances. Indeed, it is uncertain whether these factors will ever be able to be completely separated in an individual.

The experiential narratives are a good medium for cultivating understanding and recognition, but they fall short of indicating the limits of the phenomenon of 'dyslexia'. These can never be fully deduced from stories such as these, as it will not be clear to the reader whether the fact that Peter dawdles over his food has anything to do with his dyslexia.

For this reason we thought it right to supplement the stories in each chapter with a more general discussion relating to the question posed. For this part use has been made of the academic literature on dyslexia, but the argument itself has no purely scientific pretensions. It is intended more as a crystallisation of what has gone before, and aims to bring into better focus the picture of dyslexia that is starting to develop, perhaps linking together the rather diffuse experiential facts more clearly.

Once a problem has been presented more clearly at the end of each chapter by means of complementary general and specific information about aspects of dyslexia, the question is, of course: 'What are we to do about it in practice?' This question is partly answered in the first sections of each chapter, as the experiences related tell of the responses to the problems in that special case and how solutions have been sought. And the more academic sections also offer perspectives and suggestions for action. Nevertheless, a great many questions remain. We have selected the commonest ones and put them to specialists, so that at the end of each chapter you will find both questions and answers.

You may find answers to the questions that remain in more specialised books. But there are undoubtedly also a great many questions to which there are as yet no answers, and to which answers will perhaps never be found. These are also questions which this book aims to raise, and they have to do with surprise and wonder at the diverseness of people, with confusion at the fact that they are categorised as 'dyslexic' on the one hand, whilst on the other hand as individuals they are incapable of being pigeon-holed. And with a vague feeling of dissatisfaction at the fact that you can perhaps best get the meaning of a phenomenon such as dyslexia across by not being too clear and exact.

This book aims to raise this and similar questions, without encouraging the illusion that it will be able to answer them; for people who think they know everything very precisely often respond in a rather impersonal and detached way. But those who can continue to put questions to themselves about dyslexia will probably also have an understanding of it. And this book may well show that that above all is what dyslexic children need.

Saskia van der Stoel
Boazum, January 1987

CHAPTER 1

What Actually is Dyslexia?

Is Dyslexia a Closely-Defined Concept?

Dyslexia: it means literally not being able to (learn to) read properly. In practice it always goes hand in hand with dysgraphia: not being able to (learn to) spell properly.

But what do these words tell us? Nothing about the causes. Nothing about the question of what we can do about it. Nothing about how we can live with it. The only thing they suggest is that a reading and spelling problem of this kind is a precisely defined entity, that one can be clear about who is dyslexic and who is not.

The following story which Bram's mother tells shows that things are not always so simple. Bram never officially had the label 'dyslexic' applied to him. But nor has anyone ever clearly said that he is not, or what in fact is the matter.

In any case, to the Remedial School (LOM school)* and to his mother Bram is just Bram. His mother says: 'So long as he's happy', and the Remedial School says: 'After all, we did teach him to read. So why should we stick a label on him?'

What do the experts say? They say: 'This is a borderline case'. There are aspects of the story of Bram which point in the direction of dyslexia as a pure concept but there are also arguments which militate against that diagnosis.

So reality does not always fit into the frameworks we want to force it into. It is too mobile, insufficiently tangible. In order to have something to get hold of, academics try to record reality in definitions. They limit a definition and say: 'This is dyslexia and that is not'. They draw boundaries and try to agree on them. This is necessary to be able to think of things of this kind. But if your child is characterised in this way it is well to realise

1

that this will never pigeon-hole him completely. It says a number of things about him but by no means everything. It makes his problems more understandable. The word 'dyslexia' is a handle, no more.

The Story of Bram (Aged 10) Told by his Mother

WHAT DID I DO WRONG EARLIER?

I had a normal confinement, but I have heard that things sometimes go wrong earlier. In about the sixth month of pregnancy, I think, when the left and right halves of the brain develop. That's when something goes wrong. So from time to time I've wondered: What did I do wrong in that sixth month? I was simply working in a laboratory. Have I been exposed to radiation or something like that?

Bram was the first child, so I didn't have much to compare him with. Children in the neighbourhood, of course. According to insiders and outsiders they were all much more clever and deft. It made me completely frustrated, and I wanted to say: Just look at my child! One day I thought: I simply won't indulge in that. And that's how it still is; I've no need to compare him.

All the same you intuitively feel something is not quite right. When he was six months old, for instance, I kept thinking: How lethargic he is, how feebly he responds. Not really an active child, but always busy in one way or another. When he sat on his rocking chair he would always sway backwards and forwards with his hands and feet. An irregular flapping motion. If you put something into his hands it was fine. It never struck me as being anything special until an acquaintance of mine said: 'In my opinion there's something wrong with him'. Only then did I dare admit that that is what I had thought all along. But if you say something like that to, say, your husband, he immediately thinks you are an overconcerned mother.

So when Bram was just under a year old I took him along to a doctor one day. He did all the standard tests and said: 'Admittedly he won't be a professor, but...' Someone like that can only determine exact things and for the rest you've nothing to go on. I thought it was so one-sided! But I thought: well, we shall see. Things didn't go all that well with crawling and so on either. He never really crawled, he shuffled along on his buttocks with his feet together. It was terribly funny to watch, but if I had known then that that had something to do with it, of course I would have taught him to crawl. At that time I went to the physiotherapist about my knee, and I told him about the crawling. He said: 'Take him onto the bed sometime and roll him about a bit. Romp with him and do some little exercises together.' But I didn't do so; perhaps if I had things would not have gone as they did. When I see now the physiotherapy they give at the Remedial School, I say to myself: 'Yes, that really does help.'

When he was about eighteen months old I went on a course somewhere, I wanted to live a little for myself again. Fortunately in the same building there was a child-minder, with a collection of other children. So I left him there. But it was impossible to calm him down when I left him. At the time I felt that I had to persist, but later you think: gosh, if only I had acted differently. But it wasn't altogether possible.

And he would fall. He really would come a cropper. Always slap bang forwards or backwards. He didn't break his fall using his knees or hands. The times he fell on his head... Perhaps something was damaged then. What happened the first time? That is what you don't know. Anyhow his motor skills were not well developed. Going upstairs, for instance. He would always drag one foot behind, you know, on the same stair. He never put it on the next one. Early on, of course, little ones all do that but when they get to be about three... In fact Bram still often trips on the stairs. In addition it was always a mess at the table, overturning beakers and so on. And later at the Remedial School you heard people say: 'But do you know what that means?' At nursery school things actually went very well. He liked it there and played well with the other children. But the teacher said to me: 'He's always having these moods. One time he'll do something and the next time he won't'.

NOTHING FALLS INTO PLACE!

Only at primary school did the fun begin. There was a teacher there who had years of experience, but I thought her so hard. It was something like: 'Right, now all do it like this, then we'll do this'. Bram sat at a table and was being given instructions which he couldn't carry out at all. Tears! When I went to collect him I would say to the other children: 'Where is Bram?' 'Oh, he's crying in the classroom. He's still got to clear this up or he hasn't yet finished that... Or the teacher has said this or that to him.'

After a little while he didn't want to go to school at all any more. And I thought: what is this all about? What is one to do? Perhaps I should have simply have kept him at home a little longer, I now think. But at the time you think it will all blow over.

Fortunately the teacher became pregnant and left. And we got a teacher — well, she's suffering from nerves, she's actually always overwrought, she simply can't cope with a class of 40 children. But she's a treasure, really nice. She had absolutely no experience and came to a class of 22 boys and four girls. A disastrous combination, as all those boys were terribly naughty. Nice, but troublesome.

I told her how difficult things were with Bram and she said: 'Well, let him just potter about a bit for the time being. Then we'll see.' And as that year progressed he became a happier and more cheerful child. He no longer needed anything. Everything went swimmingly. Because actually they have to work quite a lot, you know, at a nursery school like that. They really work! Some children can cope with that perfectly well, but Bram happened to be one who couldn't. They then simply didn't do any more with him as regards the essentials for primary school.

After that peaceful year we decided to keep him with that teacher, as nothing was falling into place. For example, right up to the end he was still doing scribbles. Counting and nursery rhymes were not there at all. He wasn't actually progressing. We had absolutely no comparison, but of course a child must make progress! For the third year at infants' school he got a different teacher, with twelve children in the class. We agreed that she would keep a close eye on him. There was one other boy, who later went to the ZMLK* school. And she was really able to do a great deal with those two children, in that small class. She was able to observe them well.

BRAM DOES NOT ACQUIRE ANY BASIC LANGUAGE SKILLS

A day came when the Schools Advisory Service (SBD)* came into the picture. A lady came along to observe him in class. She told me that there was indeed something wrong. Well, of course I had known that all along! A psychologist would be brought in. He came; a man who of course was a total stranger to Bram. So Bram simply wouldn't leave the class! This man also had absolutely no knowledge of how to handle children tactfully — he was a dreadful fellow.

After all, the matter was becoming urgent, as by now the Whit holiday was on us and still nothing had been decided. You have to imagine the situation, all the children were saying: 'We're going to Mr Beukenkamp's class' (the first primary school class). And Bram was asking: 'Mummy, am I going to Mr Beukenkamp's class as well?' It was difficult for me to say 'yes'! After all, I half knew there was no way it would be possible. Then my sister said to me — she'd been faced with this situation more often, she is a psychologist — 'Soon the Remedial School will be full and then they'll say: "Send him to the first primary class first, just for six weeks".' She said: 'Do you know what you should do? Simply register him at the Remedial School!' That's what I did. I had a discussion with the head of that school and she said: 'When I hear the story as you're telling it, you should have come to us straight away.' But who could have told me that if the Schools Advisory Service and the nursery school teacher didn't? You don't know the right route. They're all working completely at cross-purposes.

But I still didn't dare decide, as long as the psychologist had still not done his work. Fortunately the Remedial School understood all this. They said: 'Just wait for things to happen

and don't worry; as soon as he has been we will go into action.'
Eventually in due course the test was administered and we were
invited to a discussion, my husband and I. The psychologist
said: 'Well, things don't look all that good.' I said: 'We already
suspected that.' It turned out that he was aware that we had put
Bram down for the Remedial School, but I told him that we had
been awaiting his findings before making a definite decision.
'Well,' he said, 'you can go ahead now, although in my opinion
he would be better suited to an MLK School.'* I said: 'But that
is another level lower, and in my opinion his intelligence is normal, so to me that doesn't seem sensible.'

For Bram was able to pick things up very well. He was
extremely interested in all kinds of topics. Old houses and old
ships, for example. 'What did that used to be like, mummy?' I
certainly didn't have the feeling that things were above his head.
He always used to be worried about all kinds of things. Then he
would sometimes say: 'I hope I don't quickly get to be a hundred, as then I'll die.' Thoughts of that kind were absolutely typical of him. And because he reflects on everything in that way, a
certain threshold is raised from time to time, I sometimes think.

Sometimes he simply makes problems where there aren't
any. Just recently, for instance, he was to take his swimming
certificate, the third. Swimming with clothes on. 'But mummy,
how do you do that?' I explained it to him: 'Well, first you put
your swimming trunks on, and over those your underpants,
your sports shirt, your trousers, socks, boots and so on. And
then you go into the swimming pool.' 'I just don't get it at all!'
'Well,' I say, 'just quietly and calmly think it over.'

We set off and half way to the swimming pool he suddenly
says: 'I know.' Of course, I say: 'What?' 'Well, what you are
supposed to do in the swimming pool.' So all that time he had
just been thinking, trying to imagine it to himself. And that's
how it is with a lot of things. He often gets angry if he can't
understand something immediately and then he sits there endlessly brooding over it. Whilst another child will perhaps not
try to imagine it in such a precise way. But if he is angry his
whole concentration is gone... That's what I always told the
Remedial School: make sure he does not get angry.

But all the same, in spite of his ability to reflect thoroughly on things, at the nursery school he had done hopelessly in the test. The psychologist showed me the exercises: 'He wouldn't do that one at all. We didn't get as far as this one, he set his face completely against that one and he spent far too long on that one.' I looked at my husband. His face was so long! Afterwards he said: 'I aged ten years in that half hour.' He hadn't been prepared for it at all, as I had been.

Whilst the psychologist was busy explaining all this I thought: Oh dear, my little Bram, there you go. But we said: 'What exactly is the difference between an MLK School and a Remedial School? And what are the options after that?' Those are the sort of questions you ask; crazy really! And at the words Individual Technical Education (ITO)* the colour went from my husband's face. But the psychologist explained it all admirably. He didn't put any label on him, but told us the hows and whys of his advice: Bram had very poor concentration and in addition had acquired no recognisable language skills.

But he talked and chattered well, in fact he always has done. Certainly if you compare him with his younger sister: she chattered really clumsily and stuttered. One difference is that at the nursery school Bram never picked up a word of the dialect that is normal here. A lot of children in his class spoke it, but that language didn't affect him at all. And that is a difference compared to my daughter: she comes home now with a thousand and one new words.

But to finish the story about the psychologist from the Schools Advisory Service: my sister had also warned me: 'remember to ask for that test report! Otherwise he'll disappear with it and then you won't know anything.' So I did that. Admittedly he said: 'It isn't normal', and 'Are you sure you'll be able to read that?', but I got it. I read it; there was a little report in it: 'Child taken out of the class under stress.' They ought to test the little children with their parents or the teacher present!

Well, there I sat. So my husband said: 'I've aged ten years' and went back to work. And I actually had nobody to pour out my heart to, to get my thoughts in some sort of order. For a time I did in fact talk about it a great deal, because I didn't want to bottle it all up. But I've been really shocked by most people's reactions. One said, 'Goodness, and he actually looks really normal!'

BRAM IS OF AVERAGE INTELLIGENCE, BUT THERE IS MUCH THAT HE CANNOT GRASP

As soon as possible I then cut through the knot and rang up the Remedial School. And it was really fantastic: within a few days the teacher rang back with all the appointments that were necessary: with the doctor, the psychologist, the head of the school, and another body we had to have a discussion with. This turned out to be the admissions committee. The procedure was set in motion and within two weeks everything was behind us.

Once we knew for certain that Bram was not going to the ordinary primary school, I said to him: 'Bram, just listen to me. You've now done that test, and it didn't go very well.' 'No, mummy, I couldn't manage it at all. I didn't know what I had to do, I simply didn't get it!' And I said: 'I think you'll be going to school in the town', as we still weren't absolutely certain about it. They had said: 'If the assessment shows that we can do something with him, he'll be welcome.'

During that time, all the children in Bram's class went to see Mr Beukenkamp one afternoon to get to know him. He just went along with the rest, but then he said: 'I won't be coming here, though.' Yes, they were miserable times, but somehow or other you manage to come through them, that's the strange thing.

That Remedial School, incidentally, took care of us fantastically well. The first time we went along there it was like a breath of fresh air! You turn up at a school like that with the idea that first you want to see what it is like. For he is your child, and it's a strange feeling: you start to behave like a sort of tiger. Such primitive behaviour — after the manner of: if you do anything wrong with him I'll tear you to pieces.

I jumped at absolutely everything during that time. I was just as sharp and catty to everyone. Yes, I really changed in that period, but it transpired that they had an excellent understanding of this at that Remedial School. You didn't need to be nice at all. An enormously enjoyable atmosphere prevailed. 'That's something I insist on', the head of the school said. And they were all able to get on so well with Bram. They didn't talk above his head at all, as grown-ups often do, but really got him involved.

We ourselves were very suspicious. We didn't dare tell them a great deal about Bram, for fear that it would come across in the wrong way. But when we came away the first thing I said to my husband was: 'My goodness, at least they're people!'

That psychologist at the Remedial School, for instance, that was such a difference! First I had asked anxiously whether it was a man or a woman. 'A man!' Oh heavens, I thought. But when he came up to us he was such a friendly type, and he said: 'I've come for Bram.' 'That's me', Bram said of his own accord. And before I knew it I saw them disappearing one after the other, down the long corridor. Bram going off with a stranger of his own accord, I could hardly believe my eyes! Admittedly afterwards he was silent for a whole afternoon with the experience of it, things like that always affect him greatly. But he had found it very enjoyable. Everything had gone off in a very playful fashion. 'Yes,' he said, 'of course I had to draw some of those stupid things on paper again. But he was a really nice man.' It took a whole morning.

The nice thing about that nursery school teacher was that she had written a little report about Bram off her own bat, and in fact that amounted to the same thing as came out of the Remedial School. She had looked after him for a year, and thought that he was of average intelligence with a boundless interest in a whole range of things. And perhaps precisely because of that there was a lot he could not grasp. But by a certain stage all the nursery school children could write their own names and Bram couldn't. Then she took hold of his hand and helped him. But before he could do that it took a further year and a half. And as for the practice that preceded that, don't ask!

HE NEEDS TO BE ALLOWED TO LEARN AT HIS OWN PACE

At any rate, both the impressions of the nursery school teacher and the tests at the Remedial School pointed to the fact that Bram would be in the right place at the Remedial School. So after a holiday during which we did all kinds of enjoyable things with him, the first day of school arrived. He was then round about seven.

Well, it was quite a carry on! That first time we took him in the car. Bram went and sat down, next to Astrid, another newcomer. Both had their heads bowed, both were in floods of tears. And the other children around them were all saying things like: 'What's your name?' But Bram was incapable of uttering a single word. Fortunately the teacher reacted fantastically and the moment came when I just left. At each window I waved vigorously. At the end of the afternoon he was brought home in the little bus. He got off and just said: 'Well, it was really ever so nice.' Nevertheless it took him a lot of effort to get used to that class, and the little bus too. There were children on it, he said, who looked so strange. Down's Syndrome children and suchlike.

Of course I had a discussion with the school advisory group. They said: 'It may well be three or four years before he'll be able to read and write.' I thought: Well, that's strange! But they said: 'We must simply be patient, we can do all sorts of things with him. Nothing in his potential has so far been spoilt and no opportunities frittered away, nobody has yet got off on the wrong foot with him. So everything will work successfully. First he must just calm down and find his feet. Things will turn out fine: we have been working here for about 20 years now, we've gradually accumulated quite a lot of experience.' That's what they said, and that put my mind at rest enormously. What I find very positive about that Remedial School is that from the start they teach the children that they are there because there is something about them which will not just go away of its own accord. 'We're going to work on that. First we learn to draw and then we make words as well and then we make little songs about it. And then you'll see that it'll all go right.' That is the approach.

They have a system: on Monday morning they do a weekend drawing. We often go sailing, so Bram drew boats, boats and still more boats. At the beginning these were very unclear and vague drawings. But it was a requirement that the drawings should be good. It wasn't merely play, it was serious. The teacher said: 'There needs to be more on that drawing.' And then gradually he started to draw more: the interior and the people on the boat. Mind you, that took quite a while. But when things had reached that stage they said at the school: 'Now it's coming.'

The teacher told me that there really wasn't anything there at the start. It all had to be brought up from the very bottom. He was at the school for about a year and a half before we began to see a little progress. And then one day he came home and said to me: 'Well, I can do it.' I said: 'What can you do?' 'I can read, the teacher said I was to tell you that I can read now.' You'll understand if I tell you I then went off to the school with a bunch of flowers in my hand!

How they teach there, that's really funny! They all sit there just writing letters in the air. I thought to myself: what sort of place have I landed up in for goodness' sake?

At the start Bram's eye and hand coordination was absolutely zero. He couldn't combine things. And if the teacher said to him: 'Bram, what does an E look like? Just go up to the blackboard and write a really big E', Bram would stand in front of the blackboard and say: 'I can't remember. I can't do it now. I daren't do it!' Then his head would drop and he would do nothing. That was the first year at the Remedial School. Then he was just eight years old. 'Well, that's fear of failure', we then said. But goodness me, how hard we had to work at that! And in my opinion that came from that first year at the nursery school, as he didn't get it from me. I never worked with him.

He is now ten and can read well, but it makes him terribly tired. Two pages, that's all. He reads *Rasmus the Tramp*, the simplified version of the book, in large print and with easy sentence structures. After those two pages I read on. And I make little books for him. The teacher now says to me: 'He's certainly got it in him for the junior technical school.'* So we simply don't look any further than that. Bram himself also says:

'Later on I'll go to the technical school, learning to work on motorbikes and that sort of thing.' He takes to technology. He is really a star in technical Lego. He only has to look at a really complicated drawing once and then he builds it from memory.

Arithmetic is also going well, although he was rather slow at it at the start. But for instance mental arithmetic, once he's got the hang of it — well, he's super-fast at it! He's already easily overtaken me. Recently he came up with a sum: 'Mummy, now we have to do 16 times 2 millimetres...' 'And do you understand that?' 'No, I don't understand it at all! Teacher said: "Bram, that little computer in your head hasn't had a good sleep. Today it's to have a day off. We'll carry on tomorrow".' And then he asks me: 'Mummy, is there really a little computer in my head, do you believe that?' I say: 'At any rate I think it does work like that. But then it's much more complicated.' 'Is there nothing you can do to alter it, then?' 'No,' I say, 'if there's something wrong you can't remake it.'

Bram can now also write reasonably well. We have bought calligraphy pens, you can write really beautifully with those, in splendid colours. He thinks that's marvellous! The only thing is, putting thoughts down on paper. There's still a block somewhere with that. It still goes very haltingly. But dictation goes reasonably well. The only thing is, he is now behaving in a very antisocial way. He swears and yells, and is extremely intractable. I thought: surely he isn't starting puberty already?

Commentary by Specialists

WHAT DOES ONE UNDERSTAND BY THE TERM DYSLEXIA?

Dyslexia is a disorder in learning to read and spell, but we do not call every reading and spelling disorder dyslexia. The name has to do with the causes which we surmise lie behind the disorder. Thus there are children who cannot learn to read or write because they lack the intelligence to do so. Other causes of learning disorders lie in brain damage, emotional, psychological and social problems, or obvious handicaps such as blindness and deafness. If difficulty in acquiring written language can be attributed to one of the above factors, by definition we do not call the disorder dyslexia.

But then what in fact is dyslexia? And related to that: what in fact is the cause of it? Or do we simply put the 'dyslexia' label on that group of children with reading and writing problems which remains after we have excluded every other conceivable cause? Is dyslexia perhaps an 'inexplicable reading and writing disorder'?

If one reads the literature on the subject, one could well come to this conclusion. Writers often state more clearly what dyslexia is not rather than what it actually is. Nevertheless in scientific circles a clearer and clearer picture is gradually beginning to emerge of a demarcated disorder under the common denominator of 'dyslexia'. But in our thinking about this phenomenon we must try to put aside all associations with 'a disease' and a related 'clearly identifiable cause'.

Dyslexia is not a disease, it is a lack of talent, in all probability inherited, for acquiring language. This hereditary aspect is no doubt reflected physically in the form of delay in the development of, for example, nerve cells. But for now this is of little importance for getting to grips with the phenomenon of dyslexia. We must simply accept dyslexia as a given characteristic, as red hair and brown eyes are. Just as 'red hair' often goes with 'freckles', however, people have sought connections which might be characteristic of dyslexia, features which make it more probable that a child will be dyslexic. Thus it has been suggested that dyslexic children experience aberrant motor development, that for example they often lack a crawling stage, but research has shown that this is no more true of them than of children who learn to read and write at school without problems. However, in the case of one in five dyslexic children disturbances in the so-called precision motor functions were found. This can manifest itself in handwriting, for example. Such children write in a very forced way. Nor do eye deviations or left-handedness occur more frequently in the case of dyslexic children than in a random sample of others, although what is striking is that many dyslexic children have a very good visual memory, sometimes even a photographic one. Moreover, they often evidence a remarkably strongly developed spatial under-standing. Nevertheless these are all areas which do not in them-selves typify dyslexia.

Only the fact that language development does not proceed in an optimum manner is typical. Dyslexic children have more difficulty than others in remembering language. This can mani-fest itself at a younger age in their continuing to talk inarticu-lately for a longer period, cannot properly remember the names of the other children in their class, or have difficulty with the words of poems and songs. Often it really only becomes notice-able when they are learning to read and write. In spite of the fact that everyone expects them to be able to learn without problems, they quickly find themselves falling behind their contemporaries in these areas. And this unexpected lost ground is actually the most typical feature of dyslexia.

QUESTIONS

Should dyslexic children be treated differently from other children with reading and writing disorders?

For every child with learning problems it is important to examine precisely where the problems arise, for example what mistakes the child makes and how they are to be avoided. Sometimes dyslexic children will make the same kinds of mis-takes as other children with reading and writing disorders. They can then wholly or partly be helped in the same way.

However, it is not only the points on which these children fail which are important, but also the areas in which they do well, for in helping children with learning disorders it is pre-cisely these strong aspects which can be put to very good use. If a dyslexic child has a photographic memory, for instance, you can try to put the spelling rules into a table; the child will be able to remember this very much better. In any case, with many dyslexic children rules are absorbed readily, as if they have a rule they do not need to feel or sense what is right but can reason it out.

Hence each approach must be grafted onto a map of the strong and weak sides of the individual child. Whether that child falls under the heading of 'dyslexic' is not so relevant.

Does the label 'dyslexia' have meaning for ordinary everyday life?

The opinions of people who work with dyslexic children differ in this regard. Many schools draw back from 'defining' a child in this way. But parents often find that this description gives them something to hold on to. It is as if in this way they can understand and handle their child's difficulties better. It gives them, as it were, an explanation for a variety of things which hitherto were obscure. In an emotional context the label 'dyslexia' can therefore be a support. This is also clear in the case of parents who can suddenly place their own 'dyslexic' past into context. People evidently experience it as a relief to be able to name the problems and reduce them to a recognised concept.

In practice too it is sensible to call phenomena by their names. Naming them can open the way to understanding, to help, to appropriate steps (for example in relation to examinations) and even to financial support to facilitate specialised assistance.

Why are the expressions 'reading blindness' and 'word blindness' hardly used at all in this book with regard to dyslexia?

No satisfactory English words have really been found for 'dyslexia' and 'dysgraphia'. The concepts of 'reading blindness' and 'word blindness' arose in a time when it was thought that dyslexia was mainly an eye problem. Children with this aberration, it was said, could not see the words properly and needed special glasses to do so. Even today there are still methods of treatment which are based on this starting point.

However, dyslexia is not a visual problem and it has never been demonstrated that this handicap can be improved via the eyes. In individual cases either no effect is reported or there is an instinctive improvement. Scientific research in various countries has shown that no measurable results can be expected from these methods of treatment. This is all the more reason to suppose that names such as 'reading blindness' and 'word blindness' can frequently put parents onto the wrong track.

Just as one must not call children who are not musical 'tone deaf', so the concepts of 'reading blindness' and 'word blindness' need to be more or less ruled out in the context of dyslexia. Parents who suspect that their child has an eye disorder are advised to have this looked into by an ophthalmist.

CHAPTER 2

The Difficulty of Dyslexia

Is Dyslexia a Problem of the School or of the Child?

Problems with reading and writing: one comes across them everywhere. Teachers complain that their students 'are unable to write proper English any more'. In secondary schools the cry is: 'He simply can't read the question'. And companies lament the fact that job applications are of a depressingly low quality.

Is it a question of dyslexia in all these cases? Is the problem far wider than one might imagine? Or can we put a number of these complaints down to the teaching? Is less attention perhaps being paid nowadays to the teaching of reading and writing?

The story told by David's parents shows that schools do not always blow situations up into major problems. If a child is not lagging behind in other areas they find themselves able to put up with reading and writing difficulties. Indeed, this occurs quite often.

The question then is: in the case of which poor readers and writers is their moderate progress due to problems in themselves as a result of which they have difficulty in acquiring these skills? Are they to be clearly distinguished from others who have simply had poor teaching? What can the school do to cater for them in the best way possible?

The Parents of David (Aged 13) tell their Story

DAVID STILL HAS TO SPELL EVERYTHING OUT

The first time we discovered that something was going wrong was around Christmastime when he was in the first class of primary school. David could not make the transition from spelling to reading, recognising parts of words. He still had to spell everything out and even this method did not always give him the right answers. As they so attractively put it, 'he could not make a synthesis from an analysis'. We had not at all expected that he would have difficulty at school, as he gave the impression of being intelligent. Nor had any problems arisen at infants' school. For instance we were never told: 'He's having difficulty with that'. Admittedly at infants' school he was fairly shy. In retrospect one might suppose that this was a form of fear of failure. But of course it is hard to say anything about that now.

There was one particular aspect of infants' school that struck us, but to which we scarcely paid any attention at the time. This was drawing. David drew in areas. He seldom actually drew shapes or pictures. And if he had to copy something he would lose the thread if he took his pencil off the paper. That was perhaps an early indication. Also in the family there are areas which point in the direction of 'dyslexia'. Except that that is always vehemently denied, both by the parents and by the teachers, in fact.

But what is one to make of a cousin who is certainly not stupid but who is in the second year of the certificate of secondary education class and has three times been kept back a year because of his level of language skills? Then you start asking yourself all sorts of questions, don't you? But OK, his parents say he doesn't work for it. You see, David cannot have got any real talent for language from us. Language was always the greatest stumbling block in our education. Actually, the sciences side suits us both much better. But of course that doesn't mean by definition that we are also dyslexic. Actually we are sensitive to language and so is David. His language skills, for example, are shown by the fact that he always notices when a sentence is formulated wrongly. If you examine it letter by letter, a sentence like that often turns out to be illogical. And logic is something David has down to his fingertips.

David can also express himself very well compared to other children. That is something he had even when he was still quite young. For instance, when he was two and a half he was in hospital for a while and even at that early stage he managed to make it completely clear what he wanted. Our second child is far from having the powers of expression which David has. She finds it much more difficult to say what she means. Perhaps as a result of that she's likely to have problems later with foreign languages, particularly as regards translating. But of course that has little or nothing to do with dyslexia.

That is exactly what we think is the difficult aspect of dyslexia: it is a sort of collective name for language problems, but in themselves those problems are not characteristic of dyslexia. They occur in isolated form, or to a lesser extent, in other people too. In our view, then, what one has with dyslexia is not a clearly defined picture. That is why the concept encounters so much resistance. If you're talking about measles, at least you know that it is associated with red spots and a fever, and you know what you can do about it. But something like dyslexia is so awfully vague.

Teachers in primary schools sometimes fail to notice it completely. After all, they have large numbers of children to cope with who all have their strong and somewhat less strong sides. Often they cannot assess that very well for each individual child, especially if the child does not otherwise have many problems. Of course as parents you find yourselves in a completely different position, as to you your own child is always a separate case.

That's how it was in David's case too. At the start we got no response at all from the school to our questions. It was put on the back burner a little, after the fashion of: 'Just be patient. His social skills are good and he is excellent at expressing himself. I expect he'll grow out of it'. In this way they came up with all kinds of things which offered a very large measure of compensation for what he actually couldn't do. Their overall impression of the boy was positive, so there could hardly be any problems, could there?

All the same, to us as parents there were all manner of things that made us think: Gosh, that's odd. For instance, as a Christmas present we once gave him a book which he ought to have been able to read in the first primary class. But things just didn't turn out that way. Nevertheless at that time we simply let things ride. We were afraid the teachers would think we were looking over their shoulders too much or were criticising their method of teaching.

David was at a Jena-Plan* school, where classes 1, 2 and 3 all sat together. Hence at a certain time he simply passed on to the second year. After the summer holiday we then saw clearly that he had fallen a very long way behind. But we were told that this happened with quite a lot of children after six weeks' holiday. So not surprisingly we thought: It must be part of the normal pattern.

People also frequently came up with the argument: 'There are children who do far worse than him'. But for the same money, of course, you can also make a comparison with the group which is doing significantly better. For example, at that school they had small groups which read together, led by a reading monitor. And we noticed that at the start of the second year, within a few weeks David was reading with a child in the first year. You see, he himself never made it into a problem. Evidently he had sufficient ability to compensate for this. In the third year, on the advice of an acquaintance, we started practising a series of words with David. We did this very seriously, but all the same with your own child you often do not have the patience you can bring to someone else's child. And in addition they react much more violently towards their parents than they would towards somebody else. Perhaps because they feel your disappointment if they are not successful.

When he was in the third class we thought of arranging for him to be kept back in that year, but no-one was in favour of that because of his emotional development. Nor could we ourselves really see how it could produce a specific improvement. The other subjects, such as arithmetic, were going very well, he had no problems with them whatsoever. And even in the area of language he was not really confronted by his shortcomings. At that school he was able to get away quite well without having to put things down on paper. Only occasionally were they required to write stories and that kind of thing. But when it did happen, he didn't get on very well at all.

Another thing which he found difficult was joined-up writing. He could hardly do that at all. On one occasion he said: 'I don't know how to make the "g"'. And it turned out that he really couldn't manage the motor movements of that letter. We then did something about that at home. We drew the letter very large in the air. Those were things he really didn't find it at all easy to crack. Also his handwriting was illegible. Really chaotic.

THE SCHOOL CAN SAY WHAT IT LIKES...

In the fourth class we thought: The school can say what it likes, but at the end of the day we really do want to know what's the matter. So we said we wanted to have David tested. After some urging, the school was in agreement with this. The test showed that David was an above-average child who was backward in language. His spatial understanding was considerably higher than his verbal capacity. Expressed in terms of IQ, he scored 130 on his spatial skills and 112 on his verbal ones. It transpired that most problems occurred when he was offered unordered and non-meaningful material. Reading words which had no meaning — that was something he just couldn't do. He had a horror of it. But he could quite often place words which were in a context. He understood the story, but when reading aloud he often read words which were quite different from the ones that were there. It was also very characteristic of him that he often confused the common and neuter definite articles 'de' and 'het'. When he was reading he could not see the difference between one and the other.

Reading books also didn't go at all well in the fourth class. He was at the level of a 'beginning reader'. But the crazy thing is that he continued to read right through those years. Off his own bat he always had a book by his bed, and we also read to him. So he never actually hated reading. That is perhaps because we have lots of books at home, and he grew up with them.

The outcome of the test was that on the basis of all these aspects David had a mild reading and writing disorder. The advice given was that he should have remedial teaching. This was soon embarked on, first three times a week and then twice a week. The teaching took place in school time, as we thought David ought not to be burdened by something like that outside school. Fortunately that did not create any problems as far as the school was concerned.

Until that test everything had been 'mother's problem'. She was the one who made a fuss about it and nobody else paid any attention to it. The school didn't, and nor did David himself as far as one could tell. But nevertheless the test did take something of a load off his mind. Perhaps he'd never really been so aware of it, but of course he was repeatedly coming up against his failings. And to our way of thinking he still has a considerable fear of failure, although it is hard to measure it.

But now it was: 'I have dyslexia. Well, so be it. At least something's being done about it'. Actually we've never noticed him finding that label annoying. Nor has he ever been teased about it at school. Sometimes we even thought the teachers were showing too much consideration for him. Then we thought: you need to urge him to work carefully. But often we also thought: 'You're all doing an excellent job, and we won't watch over you too much as David will do his best of his own accord'. So not at every school need it be such a terrible drama for a child.

Two years after the first test David was tested again to see the extent to which he had progressed. He was then in the sixth class and had a reading level corresponding to the fourth. That did actually create problems. For instance for a long time he needed all kinds of texts. His understanding of language turned out to be average, though, and he was able to concentrate well. The handicap was clearly limited to reading and writing.

We've never been able to discover whether the remedial teaching did actually help. A child, even a dyslexic child, naturally has his own development path, and you just can't distinguish the progress on that from the useful effect of the remedial teaching. But that extra attention certainly did not do any harm. With dyslexia it is also not a matter of: now we've got the right approach. It is inherent, it remains a weakness and you have to learn to live with it.

But we do think that some improvement can often be brought about, via aids to memory, mnemonics and so on. And you can cultivate a certain skill in getting round a number of problems. But in the case of many people that will only break through at a later age. If they themselves see the usefulness of it, along the lines of: 'I must do it. I can no longer allow myself to write like that', then perhaps things will go a little better. The question as regards remedial teaching is, of course: How can you stimulate what somebody *can* do in such a way that it is useful in relation to what somebody has less inclination and talent for? That, of course, is the purpose of aids to memory, mnemonics and all manner of tables, providing a 'handle' by using characteristics which are actually functioning properly.

The difficulty of dyslexia, we think, is that there are periods when things go reasonably well, but there are also moments when they go completely wrong. Then things are miles off target. Suddenly in one of David's essays there will be ten mistakes in three lines, whilst in the rest of it there will only be two. As parents, in a situation like that you tend to say: 'Goodness me, come on, just check that properly!' But that can't be done, he simply reads over it, whilst you yourself sometimes think: What's it supposed to say, for heaven's sake? But David reads exactly what he meant.

In that sense it is a disorder which really is terribly hard to understand. It is almost impossible to explain it, you simply have to experience it, as a parent or child. The most difficult thing is perhaps to undergo all this, for you can, of course, fight against it but to a large extent you also need to steep yourself in it. For example, when there is pressure it is clear that the problems are greater. Whether it is time pressure or emotional pressure doesn't make very much difference. And just you try to do something to counter it! These considerations played a part in the fact that at a certain point in time we decided to spend more time with David. In the sixth class we both saw that from that time on he would not be able to cope in secondary education, where you have an extra two languages to deal with. And this change-over from one school to the other often coincides with the start of puberty. In David's case one could guarantee it would make for a great fiasco. So we took the bull by the horns and arranged for David to stay an extra year at primary school. The striking thing was that when we told him that one evening it was as if a great weight had been taken from him. He did not yet need to go on to something new. In retrospect we think the year he didn't change classes was very good for him. He didn't learn very much extra, certainly not as far as the other subjects are concerned, but he has become more mature as a result of it. We have the feeling that after that year he was more confident in his manner. We've also wondered from time to time whether that repeated year was a pause for breath for him, or whether it was a form of 'not tackling the problem', as he did in fact have difficult spells during that time, certainly when his whole group went to secondary school and he stayed behind. He went through a very deep valley then. There were never scenes at home, but you couldn't fail to notice that something was happening. He would then withdraw to his bedroom and often didn't have the slightest glimpse of where he was to go from there. He felt that 'I'll never learn it'.

DAVID'S PROBLEM

We think David is now comfortable, at secondary school. The question is, of course, what the future holds. He'll be there for just a little longer. It is fairly difficult to say much about it, but he'll probably need more time for certain things, particularly languages.

We informed the school of David's problem. As a result of the publicity which has been given to this subject recently, schools are in general presumably starting to have a better understanding of this kind of handicap. For instance, the head of this school is receptive towards it. He would like to offer help, but the school does not have the resources to do so. They do not get any facilities for giving extra lessons and so on. In addition there is often a lack of knowledge about the best possible ways of teaching these children. And if you are going to be realistic, in the case of many individual teachers the will is also lacking. In the case of dyslexic pupils, on parents' evenings one still gets descriptions such as 'stupid' and 'lazy'.

What is held against David — his written work shows this very clearly — is that with French and English he doesn't write the words down properly. But it often turns out that he does know them. He has learnt them properly, but simply cannot grasp the word picture. He spells the words as they sound, phonetically. And the teachers haven't noticed this at all.

For example, the French teacher has still not realised that in David's last homework there was only one word he did not know. One might say: 'Have an eye for that and simply tell the boy that, instead of returning the homework covered in red crosses and with a 1 at the bottom!'[1] This is a policy of discouragement! What they ought to be doing is paying attention to what has gone before. Every time you must only strive for what is attainable. But the difficult thing is that a child like that must not end up in such a position that his mistakes can no longer be pointed out to him.

What we saw in a piece of English homework is that a piece of Dutch text is dictated and they then have to translate it. They're very simple little sentences. But David is already busy thinking in English as he writes that Dutch down. So he can't actually work out what it says: it is half Dutch, half English. That probably has to do with his concentration, and also he simply needs to work more patiently. In our opinion dyslexia also plays a part in maths. Perhaps not immediately in the bridging year David is in, but certainly in the second class and upwards, as more text and more understanding are then involved. If you've read the question incorrectly, you're completely wrong straight away. Yet dyslexic children naturally prefer to choose science subjects. You can take it from me that there are a great many children who study the exact sciences side of the curriculum who are dyslexic in one form or another, who just muddle through with 50 to 60% for Dutch and 40 to 50% for English... But there is also another fact which has come to play a part. At a certain point in time language teaching in schools began to be carried out in a different way, and language assessed in a different way. And the point now is that if your language is not patterned in a particular way certain dyslexic phenomena will always occur, at any rate in the case of a great many children. These children are thus not actually dyslexic. There are even people who say: 'There's no such thing as dyslexia. It is all down to the teaching'. We think you're then doing a grave injustice to your children, as it's they who have to wrestle with these problems.

As far as David is concerned we're convinced the problem is of a structural nature. The fault doesn't lie with the teaching, it really is in him. For that reason we are simply letting the remedial teaching continue, also in the transitional class, as it really is needed, although his teacher initially thought that David was getting on very well. He did not immediately let her realise what the situation actually is, namely that he has major problems with the languages. She was therefore shocked recently when we showed her David's homework and written work. She said: 'He must face up clearly to the fact that things are by no means as good as they might be, as only if that awareness breaks through will he start to work more carefully of his own accord and check his work better'. So what we are now waiting for in David's case is on the one hand a form of awareness of his dyslexia and on the other hand acceptance of it. A great deal will depend on this in the years to come.

Commentary by Specialists

IT IS IMPRINTED IN THEM, BUT...

Like all children, dyslexic children too have their strong and weak sides. They are born with them, it is in them, so to speak, even though in the case of babies and pre-school children one often doesn't notice it so much. Only later does the 'aptitude profile' become clearer, and often parents recognise different aspects of it. Then they say things like: 'He gets that talent for knocking things together from grandpa', or 'I wasn't all that good at language skills when I was at school either'.

But heredity is not the only thing that determines a child's development. And this is fortunate, for otherwise everything would be completely fixed from birth. Then all one would have to do would be to give the child enough to eat and drink and just await events. Although there have been philosophers who have credited upbringing with little value, current thinking is that the environment in which a child finds itself also counts for a great deal. Hence the ultimate outcome is determined by the combination of an innate talent and the way in which the environment responds to it.

So you can imagine that reading and spelling problems will arise if a child of normal aptitude is not given adequate teaching in those two areas. But conversely it is also possible, in spite of good teaching help, that a child will not learn to read and spell fluently. In that case he or she simply has no aptitude for it.

With dyslexic children, this last is the case, though this is not to say that the school cannot contribute towards solving the problem. It is precisely dyslexic children who ought to be given the best reading and writing teaching possible. In contrast to children who are very gifted in these areas they will never learn to acquire a command of these skills by means of a play approach.

The mistakes which dyslexic children make, however, do not always differ in principle from those of children who have had poor language teaching. But they do often make more errors, and the ones they do make are more incomprehensible and intractable. They are not so easily unlearnt. Nevertheless one cannot conclude on the basis of the child's mistakes alone whether he or she is dyslexic or not. But if a normal intelligent child, who otherwise has no handicaps or problems worth mentioning, is seriously backward at school in reading and writing, one's thoughts ought to start to turn towards dyslexia, as in such a case where can the problem lie except in a deficient aptitude?

QUESTIONS

Should dyslexic children be taught by different methods from non-dyslexic children?

In principle any child will benefit from a clearly structured method of teaching. Often, however, dyslexic children's strong and weak sides are more clearly apparent, and it would be a good idea if this could be taken account of in their teaching. But these children also differ enormously amongst themselves, so that a method specially devised for them has to be applied individually to each child. There is nothing for it but to analyse separately the specific problems of each dyslexic child so that on the basis of the problems one can decide which teaching approach will work best. In most cases it will only be possible to achieve this by bringing in extra help for the child.

Can dyslexia be coped with in part by letting children repeat a year at school, so that they can follow the language teaching better?

In individual cases it is indeed sometimes advised that a child should repeat a year. In general, however, one cannot say that such a step will produce useful results, for a dyslexic child has at least a normal aptitude for subjects other than language. If given a year longer, he or she will therefore not learn many new topics in those areas. And as far as language and reading are concerned doing a year over again still does not guarantee the approach tailored to the difficulties which the dyslexic child needs. On the contrary, an extra year doing the same thing generally means a year making the same mistakes.

If the decision to repeat a year is nevertheless still being considered, it will generally be with an eye to the emotional development of an often heavily burdened child. If a pupil repeats a year, it is advisable to use the extra year profitably by letting him or her work through a learning programme oriented towards the problems. It is best if a programme of this kind is compiled by specialists — the Schools Advisory Service or a remedial teaching specialist.

Are there dyslexic children who simply cannot learn to read and write?

At the moment it is assumed that every dyslexic child can learn the basic principles of reading and writing, at any rate to an extent which will enable them to get by in life. No child need remain illiterate. However, many dyslexic children do continue to experience their handicap as a serious obstacle. There are those who in spite of specialist help never attain the criterion of automatic reading by the third primary school class. 'Automatic reading' is reading exactly what is there, a certain pace being maintained. Very many dyslexic children turn out not to be able to learn to do this — though this is not always very obvious, as they do manage to pick up the core information from a text. And this latter, 'reading with comprehension', is, of course, more important for functioning in a social context than being able to read a text out loud.

In addition, extensive practice and a number of little tricks make it possible to skirt round quite a lot of the obstacles. In spite of the fact that some of these children will never in later life be able to write a letter free of mistakes, they can get by with the written word where, for instance, it is a matter of writing and reading a shopping list. And although the subtitles on TV films flash past too quickly for some of them to be able to follow them accurately, they will be able to make out enough to understand the gist of the story. In this way they are able ultimately to meet the minimum requirements in the areas of reading and writing.

NOTE TO CHAPTER 2

1. The Dutch marking system goes from 1 (very bad) to 10 (excellent). Failure is 5, a 6 is satisfactory.

CHAPTER 3

Being on the Alert

What are the Very First Signs of Dyslexia?

Is dyslexia a problem that is only discovered at school? Or might it be possible to identify this handicap at a younger age? When can you see for the first time that your child might later encounter difficulties in reading and writing?

These are the questions Merel and Wolf's father finds himself having to face once he found out that in most cases dyslexia is hereditary. If you yourself are dyslexic, there is therefore a chance that your children will be too, and if you yourself have experienced what it means to be dyslexic you will want to spare your children the problems, or at any rate you will be intent on making sure they do not play too dominant a role.

Merel and Wolf's father was therefore on the alert and paid close attention to the early development of his children. And his story does indeed show that even at a very young age children can differ enormously. But from those differences can you make predictions with any degree of certainty regarding a child's later development? What early phenomena are in fact directly connected with 'learning' at school and what characteristics would it be better to assign to your child's personality? Or is it not possible to separate the various factors clearly?

In spite of the required theoretical developments in this field, it transpires that it is still difficult even for academics to make statements on the basis of early childhood characteristics concerning possible dyslexia in relation to an individual child. In general, however, a good deal is known about language development and the conditions it must fulfil if a child is to be able to learn to read and write.

The Father of Merel (Aged 10) and Wolf (Aged 8) tells his Story

MEREL HAS A SORT OF FEELING FOR LANGUAGE

We had children late, in other words when we were already over thirty. First a girl, who very much resembles me in appearance but is more like her mother in her way of thinking, and then a boy. With him it was just the opposite. If you were to look at him you would say: 'He looks just like his mother'. But he resembles me tremendously in his manner of doing things.

So particularly in his case I was very eager to notice whether he was able to get on well with his contemporaries. Not that I used to be really backward, but all the same I did always have great problems at school. At primary school I did one year over again, but otherwise I actually remember little about it. It is a part of my life that I have evidently closed the door on, and perhaps it is better just to leave it like that.

At secondary school it finally transpired that I was dyslexic. There was a really nice teacher — a French lady — who said: 'Something's amiss. This boy gets high marks for all his oral work, but he's never managed more than 4 out of 10 for his written work'. Things therefore went completely wrong at that school. On two occasions I didn't go up to the next class. They said I was lazy and so on.

When after a test it turned out that I was dyslexic, I was prescribed prismatic glasses, which of course I never wore. You just don't do that at that age, do you? You see, it's very doubtful whether that would in fact have helped. From everything I hear about it now, I think one can deduce that that method of treatment has been superseded. At any rate, I struggled through that school, for ever falling over and picking myself up again. Going to school was a real hell for me.

Later I started to look into dyslexia rather more deeply, and that is how I realised it was hereditary. As far as that goes, I have never really worried about Merel. As I've already said, she's just like her mother; she has a sort of feeling for language.

She chattered early on — the first few little words at eight months, and then gradually more and more. When she was two and a half she started to copy her name and it was not long before she was announcing everywhere that there was an 'm' in Merel and an 'm' in Mummy.

When later she realised that this was the same 'm', a whole new world opened up for her. On her fourth birthday my parents gave her a book of pictures with the words underneath. And she would sit there reading this for long spells at a time. We never needed to stimulate her to do this, and indeed we didn't have all that much time to do so. We both work. But at a certain stage we noticed that she knew a large number of letters, from which — again without very much help — she made little words.

We have kept little notes of hers from that time. From the motor point of view she could scarcely manage all the letters and in particular the 'e' is repeatedly upside down or reversed. But all the same when she was four and a half she was writing: 'Dear grandpa from Merel'. And so, pretty well unnoticed, she picked up how to read and write, so that by the first class of primary school she was already a good way ahead. In fact she's still a very precocious pupil.

What was particularly striking in her case was how analytically she set to work. I still remember when she had only just got that 'reading book' and came across a picture of a cat. 'P, u, ss, y' she said immediately, but that didn't fit because it said 'cat'. She knew the 'p', because by now she could write 'papa' and 'mamma'. And that word 'cat' didn't start with the 'p'. 'What letter is that, daddy?' she then asked me, pointing to the 'c' of 'cat'. And that is how she worked out that it said 'cat' and that the last unknown letter must therefore be a 't'.

She set to work in the same way when she had to draw at infants' school. She found that delightful, but was not particularly good at it. She couldn't draw something just like that but always had to reflect about it. The roof of a house, for instance, just a triangle which the other children drew freehand; with her, if she didn't pay attention it almost became an arc. So what did she do? She devised a way of drawing it.

First she draw a horizontal line, let's call that the base, and marked the ends of it with dots. Then she placed a dot above that line, in other words the top of the triangle, and then joined those points up. That's how she drew squares and other geometrical figures too: by analysing what they actually looked like and then building them up out of their components. She couldn't do it instinctively.

A DIFFERENT STORY WITH WOLF

Well, as a result of all those aspects I never actually had any fears that Merel would encounter difficulties with reading and writing. But things were different with Wolf. I instinctively recognised a great deal in him early on. Things which perhaps do not have anything to do with dyslexia as such, but as a result of which I nevertheless thought: this needs keeping an eye on. There is much that I cannot put into words. Let me put it like this: it was simply that he had my pattern of reactions. For example he responded in a very fundamental way, instinctively. Not in a secondary manner like his mother and Merel. You never had the feeling he was distancing himself from things. But I found the most characteristic area was his language development. Let me start by saying that he didn't make a more stupid impression than Merel at the same age. In my opinion he understood everything, but it was only at a very late stage that he started to make use of the medium of language. Apart from some short stop words, until he was two and a half he didn't utter anything that made much sense. He could say 'yes', but for him 'no' was always a rather surly 'uh'.

Just like Merel, he started to say 'dada' and 'mamma' before his first birthday, but after that things stood still for a year. He knew a few little words and not much was added to those. The words he did actually speak merely took on a wider meaning. Thus 'green' became: 'Pappa-yes' and 'red': 'Pappa-uh'. He got that from the traffic lights. When they were sitting in the back of the car Merel and Wolf would say 'Yes' if I could drive on and 'No' or 'Uh' if I had to stop.

When at the age of two Wolf had learnt to say the word 'moo' for a cow, he also immediately lumped together with that 'milk' and 'milkman' and even 'udder salve'. For some reason 'small' was 'tietata' and from the intonation of that word you had to deduce whether he meant 'too little' or 'less' or 'quieter'.

All the same, as parents we managed to cope very well with this special language. In fact Wolf was able to make himself perfectly comprehensible to us, and if we didn't fully understand there was always Merel to point out to us that 'tiéta-ta tietata' meant a very small gnome; to her, her little brother's language was as easy as pie. Where Wolf lacked *forms* of expression he amply made up for it by his *means* of expression. A single word could be expressed in very many different ways and emphasised by numerous gestures. So he was certainly communicative. Just before he got under way with actual talking, at about the age of two and a half, for months he even uttered sentences which consisted mainly of 'tata' sounds, but which because of their intonation were very comprehensible. He spoke very melodically. For instance a sentence such as 'Pappa, ta ta tata moomoo?' was an abundantly clear plea for me to go out to the cows.

We did occasionally wonder whether he would ever learn to talk, as in that area he was significantly backward in relation to the other children of his age. There was a girl next door who was just a year younger but who already talked better. Of course you mustn't compare too much but these were all reasons for us to keep a close eye on his development in this area.

A period then began, however, when his talking progressed smoothly. When he was two and a half for some reason we started to sing a lot of nursery rhymes with him, and this enlarged his vocabulary greatly. He even learnt to count in this way, with the melody of a nursery rhyme as something to go on. 'One, two, buckle my shoe...' and so on. It turned out that he was able to link an enormous amount to a musical structure. Sometimes he knew Jip and Janneke stories completely by heart, as long as you had read them aloud with clear differences of intonation. If you didn't finish a sentence in one of those stories Wolf often filled the gap quicker than Merel. Merel first had to think and Wolf simply had it ready, it seemed.

Yet he talked dreadful gibberish for a good while longer. But we were glad that at least he was using our words. Except for the children in his class — he didn't seem to be able to remember their names, except for one, Jan. For some time he called them all 'Tommanam'. We never understood why he did that and how he came by that name. There was no Tom in his class.

Just like Merel, he was always very fond of books and of being read to. Often he would concentrate hard, reading from a picture book, murmuring aloud but sometimes incomprehensibly what was evidently a story. This was characterised by a real reading aloud tone, with very many differences in pitch. But unlike Merel he never had the inclination to want to read and understand real letters. If in an old reading book he saw the picture of the cat, he would say: 'Pussy' without regard for the word underneath. And I must say: for a child of four I don't think that is anything other than normal.

Nor can I say that at infants' school there was any particular difference between him and the other children. Of course every child is different at that age. And you always see a great deal more in your own child than in somebody else's. But all the same: he was a very normal child. He was more on a par with the others than Merel, it seems to me, because Merel was clearly ahead at that age. On the other hand he could also do things which Merel could not do so well. So when Wolf was at a certain age I forgot about it for a while. I thought I'd simply got it into my head because I myself suffered so much from dyslexia.

WOLF'S 'WEAK POINTS'

However, when Wolf was in the first primary school class, I again got that anxious feeling that 'something wasn't right'. He didn't immediately fall behind, but I did have the idea that he was not picking it all up that quickly. He was at a Montessori school and to a certain extent you're allowed to say what you want to do on any particular day. So he was able to get out of doing too many things which he couldn't manage very well. Wolf is just like me, a type who will latch onto what he actually is good at.

At a certain moment we therefore grasped the nettle and had him tested by a private institute, although it was only to set my mind at rest as far as that went. You need to bear in mind that he had then been at that school for perhaps two months and so far there was hardly any evidence of him reading or writing.

I don't know whether it's possible to establish definitely whether somebody actually is dyslexic at that age. At any rate, in Wolf's case a day of thorough testing did not give any clear indication. It was hard to prove that there was something wrong, and there was therefore an unwillingness to put a rubber stamp on him.

Yet there were indeed things which pointed to the possibility that he would have difficulty with reading and writing. For instance, he could not analyse a word into sounds, so he could not spell that word from what he heard. He had as yet no idea that each letter represents a different sound. And all the tests showed that his powers were such that one could indeed expect that at that age.

We were therefore advised not to wait but to get to work immediately, to give extra practice to certain weak points, even before he would come across them in the lesson material. We consulted with the school about this and although initially they were not all that receptive to it, finally in the second class it was provided. Thanks to the school doctor and the Schools Advisory Service we managed to arrange for him to have reading lessons by the look-and-listen method.

This is a system in which the child hears the words through headphones and simultaneously also sees them in a book. It is thought that this creates a better link between sound and image, and we also have the feeling that it really does help. At any rate Wolf does now read. He's just finished another fat Guus Kuier book. A few pages every day. Then I think: it has all been effective, as — at any rate so far — he has never taken a dislike to reading and writing. Also the school is now completely won over to this method. Eight of the 120 third-class pupils have now had lessons using the headphones.

Spelling is a completely different matter. I feel that that still hasn't properly got off the ground. When I see the sorts of mistakes he makes, now and then I really panic. My thoughts are something like: 'How on earth is he going to make any progress from that?' but then again I think to myself: At least he's writing. He himself has hardly any problems with the fact that he makes so many mistakes. And I must admit, just as we used to understand what he meant with his strange language, so we now understand what he writes. He has a complete disregard of the rules of spelling and you can often find the same word written in three different ways in a piece. But it's clear what he's trying to get across.

Who can say whether there won't be an improvement in the spelling, once he's willing to see his mistakes? Because that, in fact, is what he doesn't do at the moment. If he writes something, he just writes it. But he will never write a rough version first or check it. He simply won't analyse his own work, and so in one fell swoop he writes in Merel's poetry album: 'Deer merel i luv you and ill stay tru to you', and she'll keep that all her life...

In these aspects too I recognise much of myself in Wolf. I too hardly ever read my work over. I'll write a letter or note without pausing for breath and then I'll get somebody else to check it over, because the moment I start to think about the words — the spelling — I can't get my thoughts down on paper properly. Then I just can't get the sentence construction sorted out. And Wolf probably has that problem too. I think the most important thing at the moment is that Wolf enjoys going to school. Right from the start I myself didn't enjoy it. That's also why I got so worried about the possibility of dyslexia in Wolf's case. But I do think, now we actually know it, that we can deal with it a lot better. As soon as something goes wrong we're there in a flash. Then we can meet the problem halfway. Who knows how much misery we've already been able to avoid by not sending him to one of those old-fashioned cramming schools and by offering him that look-and-listen method in school time. You can never say afterwards how differently things would have turned out, but all the same I'm very glad we were on the alert with Wolf.

Commentary by Specialists

LEARNING IS A CONTINUOUS PROCESS

Learning starts right from birth. Of course, a child is not born like a blank sheet of paper: he or she has a standard repertoire of reflexes, and has the necessary senses even if they are not all yet functioning fully. On the basis of the experiences received via this equipment in this new environment learning finally begins. This takes place by means of grouping and regrouping experiences. In combination with the still maturing nervous system, through this active ordering of experiences the baby begins to acquire more of a hold on its environment. It starts to recognise things and to realise that it itself is something. Finally the moment comes when the parents say to each other: 'Now he's becoming a real person'.

Perhaps this continuous and active learning process is one of the most typical characteristics of being a human being. However, to an important extent it also means that people are formed by that learning. A child which grows up in an environment rich in stimuli will develop very differently from the same child which has fewer opportunities to gain impressions. Yet children in the same environment, in the same family, often undergo a completely different development. They react differently to the same events. Each child, as it were, isolates what is its own from the totality of the information offered. For ultimately each child is a different being from the start, equipped differently from its brothers and sisters. And whereas these differences are not yet very striking in the case of very small babies, they start to evidence themselves clearly in the case of toddlers and infants' school children.

Hence it is possible to apply a standard list for the very smallest, according to which normal development ought to proceed. Both a baby's weight gain and repertoire of behaviour should meet those norms within fairly narrow limits. But for bigger children one can only indicate the normal development in a very global way. It is clear, for instance, that every normal child must sooner or later start to walk. But one will do so at 11 months and another will wait a few months longer. Both children fall within the normal range, and there is no reason to become anxious about either of them.

So when ought you, in fact, to become anxious about the development of your child? Specialists do not have any cut and dried answer to this, as it sometimes turns out that a toddler or infants' school child will spontaneously make up for even clear instances of backwardness in development. It is true that learning is a continuous process, but it progresses in fits and starts; there is acceleration and braking. It can even happen that at a certain period (for example when they are sick) children will regress to a previous phase in their development. Then they suddenly seem to have lost a whole body of achievement. In general one can therefore say that individual development in children can deviate considerably without it being possible to make concrete predictions regarding the child's later life, and in particular regarding learning at school. Only children who are very clearly backward or precocious are identified in practice, and in those cases it is therefore nearly always evident that something is wrong. In the case of dyslexia early recognition is a highly difficult matter. For example there are no striking behavioural characteristics in the case of dyslexic children. It is true that one often ascertains later that these children have experienced somewhat delayed language development, but one can deduce from the fact that in most cases this is established retrospectively that the deficiencies cannot really be described as striking. Many children get by until primary school because they have at their disposal enough ways of compensating for their use of language.

Infants' school teachers often accept the differences between children more than teachers at primary school do. The material at infants' school is suitable for very diverse forms of information processing. Both children who easily learn visually and those who prefer to involve their hearing in processing information are amply catered for at infants' school.

However, the primary school is in most cases oriented towards only one way of learning. To the extent that the difference between the lessons provided and the way in which a child gains his knowledge grows, such a child runs a greater risk of missing the boat. Certainly where there is suddenly such great reliance on the memory for language, it is often only now that a dyslexic child will display noticeable deficiencies. These deficiencies are often based on a number of 'language conditions' which are lacking but which at infants' school were perhaps never seen to be lacking. At infants' school the child uses language mainly in its meanings; he or she never has to understand how the system fits together in order to make him- or herself clear. Although languages consist of many different sounds (for example, 37 in Dutch, 44 in English) an infants' school child will never need to pronounce them separately. In an ordinary conversation you do not hear those sounds separately from each other.

All the same, in order to be able to read and spell properly it is necessary to be able to cut sentences up into different words and subsequently cut the words up into different sounds. A child who cannot do this properly will experience great difficulty in these subjects at primary school. It is therefore sensible to discover whether a child can actually hear words and sounds separately from each other and whether he or she is capable of remembering language separately from its meaning.

A child must therefore have a reasonably good command of a number of topics when he or she goes to primary school. For example he or she must immediately be able to retain and pronounce properly a (not too difficult) new word and not have any difficulty with the names of classmates. In addition he or she should be able to recite a few rhymes, as if they can do that they at least have an understanding of separate sounds. It is also important that they should be able to find the words in their memory, to be able to put their thoughts into words in properly formed sentences. In general the memory for language is very important. A child of that age, for example, should not be encountering any difficulty whatsoever with the words of songs and rhymes.

Hence at the end of the day it is in fact possible to some extent to determine whether a child will perhaps have later difficulties with reading and writing. This early recognition is often not very clear. Nevertheless, in the case of a child who is already at risk because, say, one of its parents is dyslexic, all these factors can form important indications. It then makes sense, of course, to have one's suspicion that there is evidence of dyslexia investigated as soon as possible by a specialist.

QUESTIONS

Can you do more about dyslexia in the case of early recognition?

It is incontrovertibly of great importance to recognise as soon as possible the fact that a child is dyslexic. In the case of some children, however, the handicap manifests itself more at a young age than in the case of others. Sometimes — in spite of the attentiveness of parents — it is only established that a child is dyslexic when he or she is at primary school. And a not insignificant proportion of dyslexic children only run up against their handicap for the first time at secondary school. Viewed with hindsight there were often indications of dyslexia at an earlier phase, but these were evidently not striking enough to represent an obstacle.

How early dyslexia is discovered is therefore connected with a large number of factors, by no means all of which one has control over. To begin with, the seriousness of the dyslexia plays a part, in other words: the extent to which the verbal capacities of a child lag behind his or her other capacities (above all the spatial-visual). In addition the child's general intelligence is important. Intelligent children have more ways at their disposal for compensating for or camouflaging their handicap for a while. The type of school in which a child finds itself also plays a role in whether dyslexia is likely to

be signalled at an early stage, as the stricter the requirements
of the school are in the areas of reading and spelling the sooner a child will stumble in those areas. And finally the attentiveness and expectations of the child's parents form an
important balancing item in the series of factors which are
influences on early recognition of the problem.

Although, therefore, one cannot say that it is the norm that
every dyslexic child ought to be recognised as such in the first
primary school class, it is nevertheless sensible to set the alarm
bells ringing at the first suspicion that there is evidence of
dyslexia. There are two reasons why it is important that one
should pick it up as soon as possible. First, early intervention
will protect the child from excessive frustration. For example, by
means of the choice of school or expert help one can tackle the
problems in such a way that the child does not suddenly find
itself bogged down at school. Secondly, it is easier to do something about dyslexia if one is alerted early. It is often necessary
almost to start all over again methodically and sytematically
imparting spelling, and this work is more suitable to a nine-year-
old's development than that of a fifteen-year-old. In principle, of
course, it is possible to improve the skills of a dyslexic child or
adult at any age, but the sooner a start is made the more misery
will be avoided.

*What requirements imposed at infants' school do dyslexic
children find impossible or difficult to meet?*

Most dyslexic children pass through infants' school without
encountering any conspicuous problems. It is not possible to distinguish them clearly from their classmates. However, research
has shown that a large number of children who later have to
struggle with learning problems give a rather 'young' impression at infants' school. This younger behaviour can be expressed
in various areas. Many such children, for example, utilise strategies which are characteristic of younger children. Their lack of
'maturity' is also evidenced in the way they perform tasks and in
their interest in school topics, in learning. In general they are perhaps more playful and more easily distracted, but this is never

very noticeable. For instance, one can never talk of it in terms of 'backwardness'.

All the same, however unremarkable this rather younger behaviour may be at infants' school age, it can bring problems for a child at primary school. Minor differences in age turn out to exercise a significant effect on the extent of success at school. Hence, for example, it has been shown that there is a clear link between the month a child is born in and his or her achievements at school. And at remedial schools there are a significantly greater number of pupils who were born in the summer months.

Summing up, we can say that the demands which are made on a child at infants' school are not so strict that a potentially dyslexic child will not be able to meet them. But the primary school requirements are unrelenting: in early September the reading and writing process starts for all children. And amongst those are the younger pupils, or those pupils who give the impression of being somewhat younger, who might later encounter learning problems. If a child falls into this risk group at that early age because, for instance, of having a father or mother who is dyslexic, it can do no harm to keep a close eye on his or her development in this area. The way dyslexia becomes apparent is always an interplay between on the one hand factors within the child — age, sex (boys are four times as likely to be dyslexic as girls!), disposition — and on the other hand factors which are separate from these: the demands which the school imposes, the teacher, the method of teaching, or the use of language by the child's parents.

Is it a good idea to give infants' school children extra practice in subjects they are not good at?

If it is apparent that an infants' school child is backward in a particular area, it always makes sense to devote attention to it. But caution is the watchword: it is useless to force children to do those things they cannot yet really do and — perhaps for that very reason — do not enjoy. Particularly in the case of an infants' school child, weaknesses can best be supported and compensated for by means of the areas which he or she *is* good in or things which he or she *does* enjoy. Using this approach, the child's natural development gets a fair chance to catch up under its own steam in the areas which are lagging behind.

In the case of very marked backwardness in development it is advisable to engage the help of an expert. In other cases the teacher will often have a good understanding of what falls within the 'normal' range of variation and will be able to advise on how necessary it is to provide extra stimulus to certain activities.

If you yourself are dyslexic, what is the chance that your child will be too?

From the scientific point of view little is known as yet about the hereditariness of dyslexia. It has been clear for a century now that dyslexia is inherited, but it has still not been possible to determine how this hereditary factor actually operates.

CHAPTER 4

Sailing into a Head Wind

As a Parent, Should You Concern Yourself with your Child's School Career?

Bringing up a child is a difficult business, as everyone will agree. The most difficult part of all is perhaps constantly coping with the rapid succession of changes which your child undergoes. Just when you think you have found the right direction, you can wager your last penny that precisely at that moment your child will embark on a fresh phase of life. And so you have to adapt once more and sail a different course.

For example, it is well known that many parents have difficulty in letting their child go. It is a big step, after all: from having full control over your child for four years, at primary school you have to give the child over to the teacher for a great deal of the time. But does that also mean you also have to give up completely that part of the child's upbringing? Is all the knowledge you have acquired concerning your child during those early years useless for his life at school? Is the separation between 'school' and 'home' really so great that it is as if the child lives in two different worlds?

Certainly where your child's life at school does not proceed without quarrels and difficulties you can imagine that as a parent you have an obligation actively to think and work with your child. If the child does not develop according to expectations or does not respond to the teaching in a standard way, then the special insight which parents have into the way their child functions can perhaps be of importance. Do professional educators pay enough attention to the intuition and knowledge of parents? How might the general knowledge which, for example, teachers have and the special knowledge which parents have supplement and support each other?

In this chapter Enno's parents cross swords with those who would have preferred to see them stay on the sidelines.

The Parents of Enno (Aged 12) tell their Story

ENNO AT INFANTS' AND PRIMARY SCHOOL

In the second class of infants' school Enno was tested by someone from the Educational Advisory Service.* His teacher thought: there is something wrong. But she could not put it precisely into words. It was very vague.

We ourselves were not involved in any discussion, only receiving the results. We went there and we were then bluntly informed that Enno was 'socially disturbed'. 'Very intelligent, no doubt he'll become a professor later on. But he cannot get on with other children. So he's always sitting in a classroom on his own reading'. That's what we were told. We were not asked anything, we were only told what *they* had deduced from the test.

After a conversation like that, you tend to slink away dumbfounded. After that, you start to reflect and you think: hold on a moment, that just isn't possible, because I have a child who is actually tremendously sociable! Even as a baby he simply wouldn't go into his cot, he always wanted to be doing something with somebody. If people came in he started to shine! So he was not at all a child who originally had social problems.

But it was true that he had acquired them at that school. The Educational Advisory Service was right in that respect. They had observed him and at that moment he very clearly had problems. We ourselves also confirmed that. In fact it eventually became so serious that he would start to yell with panic if a child so much as rang the doorbell, such an aversion did he have to that school and the children who went to it. He evidently found it enormously difficult to keep his head above water there. And that is why it gave him a feeling of safety to be at

home. But if a child rang the doorbell or just walked down the
street, he started to think: Oh heavens, now I've got to defend
myself again.

That was in the second infants' school class. In the first
infants' class he only went in the mornings, as he was still
sleeping every afternoon. At that time he always went around
with a great big bag around his neck into which he had
crammed all his toys. He took that with him everywhere, it was
a really charming sight.

His difficulties at school perhaps had nothing at all to do
with his dyslexia, that is possible. But on the other hand, his
uncle is also dyslexic and he showed exactly the same reaction
at that stage. So what is associated with the dyslexia and what
can you attribute to his character? Perhaps it doesn't matter all
that much. In any case even at that early stage it was a signal
for us that something was not right.

Of course you cannot say of that period that he was
dyslexic. After all, there was then no question of reading or
spelling. But we do remember that he had to make up sheets of
scraps, and he would cry off doing that. Perhaps a child realises
even at that stage that there are certain things he is not good at
taking part in. Learning nursery rhymes by heart, for instance.
We have a feeling that even at that time Enno was already having difficulty with that as well.

At any rate, as time passed he withdrew more and more
and in the last six months he no longer went to school. We
thought to ourselves: OK, so he doesn't go. After that, though,
he simply went off to primary school, as the Educational
Advisory Service did not see any further problems. Nor did
they give any advice, however, such as: this is the approach you
ought to adopt. You're just sent home with the problem. After a
few tests they had drawn their conclusions and that was that.

In the first class he wasn't one of the quickest, of course.
Fortunately he was able to get on better with his contemporaries.
Everything was much more structured, and that was more pleasant for him. He had a better overview. In fact it was not until the
second class that he experienced failure at reading. Then he had
to do extra reading after school and he found that dreadful. At

the end of the second year I happened to go along to the school and the teacher suddenly said: 'I don't know what it is, but in my opinion there is something that's not right with Enno'.

Now we had been tremendously alert throughout, as his uncle is dyslexic and I am too. So you are attentive to it. I therefore went home that afternoon and immediately put him down for the Remedial School. That was actually the most difficult moment of all: to take that step. In spite of the fact that in view of the family circumstances we were prepared for it. We've always said: 'If it's necessary we'll just have to do it'.

We were very clear-minded about this, but the primary school was not at all of the same view. They thought it was simply absurd. Of course the primary schools are all faced with falling pupil numbers and the teachers are fighting for jobs. But as yet people are completely unaware of this.

When I collected Enno from school on the last day before he went to the Remedial School, I was standing there at the door and a teacher came out and she said: 'Well, you're taking him with you, but you don't know what you're doing. There are children in my class who are getting on far worse!'

Well, we're two or three years further on now and those children have also gone to the Remedial School. But it was too late for them!

A 'MILD' CASE AT THE REMEDIAL SCHOOL

The crazy thing is that we never actually doubted that Enno needed to go to the Remedial School. We were more surprised by the fact that others had absolutely no understanding of when it was appropriate. The experts didn't, the teachers didn't, and sometimes the parents had even less realisation. We developed a bit of a nose for this, and if we found ourselves among our circle of acquaintances and their children, we would sometimes think: Well, things are not going too well there. And in fact a year or two later that's how things often turned out.

That is why so many children get to the Remedial School too late. Fortunately that did not happen with our son. This meant that he was the youngest at that school. He was never frustrated or anything like that, and was never really troubled by his problem. We have never had that phase when the child gets stuck fast, no one knows what direction one should be looking in and only after lots of digging is the real cause tracked down.

For the first two years Enno was at a Remedial School in the south of the country. Then we moved here and continued with the Remedial School in this town. But at both schools we noticed that there is nothing you could really call a 'special approach'. As far as teaching material is concerned, I mean. But the system works like this: children feel happier there than at the ordinary primary school. They are not forever running up against all kinds of barriers.

If you examine the method of a Remedial School, in the first phase there is nearly always a confused child who has to get used to the new school. The school tries to give the children self-confidence, enabling them to discover things they can do rather than things they cannot do. And that works excellently, they are tremendously good at that. The fact that the classes are smaller also contributes to this. The whole atmosphere at a school of this kind is clearly better.

But there is a logical continuation to this… As parents we often had the feeling that time was running through our fingers like sand. Nothing was actually happening. Intellectually the child was not being challenged at all. We thought that was such a waste! On the one hand, naturally, you have to accept that there are certain things which are difficult for a child in this situation. But surely they do also have their intellectual strong points? And if those are not stimulated, that part of the child will simply fall asleep.

At any rate that was clearly the case with Enno. And that is also the reason why we said: Now what can we ourselves do about it? In fact for us that has always been the central question. We ourselves made things very difficult by making that wish known in discussions at the school.

Of course we were immediately pigeon-holed as parents who overestimate themselves and their child. But we believe that we should rather see it like this: it is a bit like the problem

of the ambulance arriving at the scene of an accident. They start
by looking at the most seriously injured. They must be taken
away first. But the chances of success in their case are not so
great. Alternatively they could start with the less serious cases:
at least they will be walking again in 24 hours' time.

If — like Enno — you arrive at the Remedial School as a
relatively mild case, in fact nothing is done with you. You manage. Others, on the other hand, are given considerable help. For
example, Enno was always furthest on with his work, but the
other children were allowed to go to the teacher first. He was
always the last to take his turn.

It also depends very much on the teacher, as what they are
doing is very arduous. At one point Enno had a young teacher
who was very idealistic and enthusiastic. Once a week he came
to school specially an hour earlier and gave Enno extra lessons
and work which he was to do during the week. But later Enno
found himself with a teacher who was quite old and found
everything very difficult to cope with. And then if you go to the
school and say: 'Could he perhaps be allowed to do some extra
work?', you can see merely from her eyes that she's panicking
and thinking along the lines of: 'How am I going to keep up
with all this?'

Yet it remains a strange contradiction: a child with learning problems goes to a Remedial School. But instead of doing
extra work the child does less. Homework and 'tests' are almost
unknown concepts at the Remedial School, although, of course,
one Remedial School is not the same as another.

Now if a child goes to a Remedial School for, say, four
years, you can presume that the first two years are a transition.
But surely in the last years you ought to try to get as much as
possible of the primary education learning material into the
child? We all want to work towards achieving that as best we
can, not least the child himself!

WHAT IF HE HAD BEEN GIVEN ORDINARY TEACHING?

You might perhaps say: couldn't Enno have been able to
keep up at an ordinary primary school with some remedial

teaching? But I think that you would need to hit on a very special school. Through moving house we have experienced quite a number of schools, of course. And our impression is that most primary schools cannot cope with something like that, particularly in the present situation.

A Montessori school, for example. There children are not confronted by their problems all that much, because they can learn at their own level. But you are for ever hearing that it is precisely there that your children fall even further behind. For a Montessori school you need to be pretty sure of what you are doing.

And the ordinary primary school... a small example: there is a boy in the same class as our daughter, and he is clearly dyslexic. One day they had a road safety test. The school thought it was terribly important that everybody should pass, as that always happened for the last umpteen years. Well, of course, the child could not finish the questions because he has such difficulty in reading. So one child failed for the first time in goodness knows how many years. There was such disappointment in the class, in the whole school! What's more, a treat had been promised if everybody passed again... And even though everything was put right later, something of that kind is terrible for a child, of course.

I experienced something else with exactly the same child. They were going to rehearse a Christmas play. The scripts were issued: you will say this and you will say that. But that little boy simply couldn't read it properly. So the teacher said: 'Well now, my lad, you'd better not be in it'. So then he well and truly loses face!

Here is another striking example: we had the children at two different schools and Father Christmas came. At the ordinary school all the outstanding pupils were allowed to display their work for Father Christmas, to show him how good they were. So the dunces didn't get an opportunity. This was in contrast to the Remedial School, where every child was allowed to do something for Father Christmas.

So it was that even though he is only a mild case we hadn't wanted Enno to have the ordinary teaching, because a teacher may be ever so willing and have ever such a feeling for such children — let us assume that, though in practice they hardly ever know what dyslexia is — but I would also add: the primary school period is a time in which the child experiences all kinds of things about which he's really as yet unable to say anything. A child expresses himself poorly, he just lets everything wash over him. There is a great deal he cannot yet explain. That period — and this is also recognised in child psychology — is terribly important. It also permeates all his later development. And that is why it is best that children should grow up in a climate in which they can simply participate.

When Enno left the school we were advised that he was definitely not up to going to an ordinary secondary school. He must go to the secondary Remedial School. For us that was once again a reason to set our sails into the wind and say: 'First we'd like to hear better arguments put forward for that' and 'Isn't that the line of least resistance?' Of course a secondary Remedial School will have a good atmosphere. But will he also learn anything there?

I have just argued that children with dyslexia should definitely not go to an ordinary primary school, but I think that in this case things are somewhat different. The situation is this: at primary school regard is had virtually only to arithmetic and language. That actually occupies the children all day long. In secondary education that is not the case. There dictation is a very small part of all those other subjects. So if you can find a school which takes account of that, which is open to that, then I think dyslexic children ought to be able to feel at home at an ordinary secondary school.

We have now found a school for Enno, an IVO-MAVO* which is specially structured for children whose progress is not completely automatic. They always work in very small blocks, drawing a line under each block, so to speak, by means of a piece of written work. If they don't manage it they are allowed to do it over again. Extra lessons are provided for doing that. And in that way they never actually fall behind.

Most children never get back from the Remedial School to an ordinary school. Now Enno was the best in his class but he was absolutely not allowed to go to the ordinary secondary school! Of course there are some parents who swallow advice like that without a murmur. But you've only to look at how Enno gets on now! He's never yet had a fail mark. Only 8s and 9s. It makes him dog-tired, as he finds it a great effort now suddenly to have to work hard.

PRACTISING AT HOME WITH ENNO

I myself am also dyslexic, but to such a small extent that it has never actually caused me much trouble. I was very good at school. Only when we had to do dictation did I sit there desperately looking around and wondering: 'How do they know that?' If I could learn the words it was no problem at all. But people assumed that you knew it of its own accord, just like that; I couldn't do that.

I've never had any problems with reading and Enno too has really had only a few. What we actually have is dysgraphia. Enno started to read well when at a certain point we pushed the books of Heleen Kernkamp-Biegel into his hands. She translated *Alone in the World* by Hector Malot; he thought it was so lovely.

We never saw it as a problem of perception. True, for a time Enno had prismatic spectacles. But whether they were just a magic spell I can't say. We think the problem lies rather in grasping the word image. You simply can't retain the word. And if you've really been concentrating on something else you're even capable of writing your own name down wrongly. Enno has that very clearly. Something that is automatic in others, he has to concentrate on. For myself I found the solution was to write words out again. Just reading doesn't help. And if I have done that action I can remember it. Enno also has the same characteristic very strongly: the words he writes down a few times stay there much better.

And so we come back to the central point: what can you do? For once you have the idea that writing the words down helps, then you think: well, it's a matter of writing down, repeatedly, an endless number of words. And if that can't be done in school hours, it has to be done by the parents.

We therefore worked with Enno a great deal, especially when he was young. In holidays and so on. Then in the evenings we would think up little games, language games. And next morning after breakfast we would start on the games. Enno's sister joined in, as at first things didn't go as they ought with her either. She must have it a little bit, but to a much lesser extent.

We discovered a tremendous amount as a result of those little games. For example: let them write using a pencil, as it can be rubbed out and then they can make corrections. In that way at least they don't retain the wrong word picture. Because that is often what you get with children who are dyslexic. They write something wrongly and correct it but never see the whole word written correctly. What is more, if you are writing a letter to grandma it's annoying to send it with all those crossings-out. If you write something wrongly using a pencil, grandma simply won't be aware of it. Those are some of the little practical things. Teachers ought to take account of aspects of that kind too. Not a red cross with a letter corrected, but the whole word next to it.

Enno really didn't mind practising at home with his mother or father. It was sometimes even enjoyable. You give an enormous amount of attention to each other. But you have to do it so that it is immediately after breakfast. The child must not become occupied by other things. You mustn't have to shout out: 'Now Enno, come along in, we're going to practise'. With us it was a fixed activity: have breakfast, be at ease with each other. And after breakfast we would do it.

Of course, it is a condition that you have a good relationship with your child. If he has emotional problems, fear of failure and so on, you as parents are in a much more difficult situation. And we discovered that the older Enno became, the more he realised how much we wanted him to be able to do it. There is absolutely nothing you can do about that. You sit there and something doesn't go well and he notices: 'Oh dear, mummy is disappointed with me'. And then you can say something like: 'I'm not cross', but a boy feels it all the same. Then we realised that we mustn't continue with it. And then via a students' association we found a girl who would work with him, who wasn't so emotionally involved with it.

Another thing we noticed when we worked with him: the results always come at a different moment from the one you expect. You think: 'I'll practise this or that with him'. And if it doesn't succeed you sit there getting worked up. But it is simply your expectations that are at fault. You expect that it will have a direct effect when perhaps it simply works through slowly. You must work with them on a completely open basis. As soon as you start to say: 'I want him to learn that now', you'll get frustrated. A great many parents have problems with that. We did too, as he couldn't remember the colours. That was when he was still at infants' school, I think. Then we pointed out and laid out on the desk everything in the room that was red and everything that was blue. But when you'd finished he still couldn't do it. All the other children could and he couldn't. That's when, as parents, you get completely tense.

But once they are mature enough for it you suddenly realise that that exercise made sense. Suddenly they can place them. And then suddenly you have the reward for your patience.

ARE THE PARENTS COMPETING WITH THE SCHOOL?

Enno was given a very high assessment at the previous Remedial School. The person who had tested him said: 'A special child. Very bright'. So when we went to this present school, we told the head: 'We have an ordinary, intelligent child. *But* he is dyslexic'. Well, our putting it like that wasn't accepted at all. They even recalculated his IQ and triumphantly told us it was a few points lower than we thought. We couldn't in the least understand why they were making such a fuss about it. In retrospect we think it came about from them thinking: 'We must dispel these parents' illusions. They belong to those het-up people who want to drive their children to do things they aren't capable of'. What the school wanted most was to find everything out for itself, to work totally independently of the parents. But a mass of useful information is lost like that. On both sides, in fact. For instance, at the start of this school we realised that for a year Enno had been in a group where the children had been far, far older than him. This was because the school simply didn't know that Enno had gone to the Remedial School so early. In that year the teachers kept thinking: Gosh, something's amiss. And we *were* told that; we were told everything that was amiss with the child. We were really shocked, of course, as we had not noticed anything. Things were going very well at home. But at school they were saying: 'He doesn't adapt and he is quite different from the other children'. This made us quite upset. And a little while later it was casually let slip that they had evaluted Enno wrongly. No; that school was not structured to any form of cooperation and we thought that was a great pity. For instance a magazine with language games once came out. We were very enthusiastic about it and asked the school: 'What are your thoughts on that?' Well, the reaction was really vicious, along the lines of: 'They must learn at school and not at home'.

At the start we also naively asked from time to time: 'What are you doing now at school? Could we take those books home, just to have a glance at them?' We thought: then we can perhaps adjust to that material at home. But it really resembles a sort of boycott: as a private individual you can never get hold of those textbooks and work blocks. We even rang up the importers of the books, who said, 'We only sell them by the hundred to schools'.

Finally we had to resort to back-door methods to get hold of the teaching material, surreptitiously taking a look on parents' evenings: what's all that and what is it called? Trying to copy it. And all that just to be able to follow what's going on at school. To be able to help your child a little. Whereas in our opinion the school really ought to be saying: 'This is what we're busy doing and unfortunately we haven't quite completed it, but perhaps you can find an opportunity to do so'.

Instead of the hoped-for cooperation we kept running up against the same fear: 'Those parents must be restrained. They must learn to accept that their child is not what they had thought. They are only chasing after an ideal and that is their way of trying to cope with their frustration'.

They tell you: that's it, and please don't trouble yourself about it. You must never ask anything; as a parent you mustn't trouble yourself with your child's life. As a troublesome busybody you're simply kept outside the door. If you ask: 'What are you doing and what is your plan of treatment?' you are forcing them into formulating the situation and they don't actually want that. That is really very striking.

We find it so strange. If we ask the dentist questions he is pleased that we are interested in his profession and glad to explain how the various aspects relate. But as parents of a child with learning difficulties you seem to have no right to information. People are afraid you simply won't adjust to it.

But this is confusing the issue. If you want to know something about medical matters you don't yourself go and play at doctors! If you want to know about such things you don't immediately go and sit on a treatment couch. We're not a self-help group or alternative psychologists or anything like that. But it's like this: if as a parent you see that your child has had a temperature of 106° for three days and isn't drinking anything, you know you have to call the doctor. Well, I'd like to have indications of that kind in the area of dyslexia. That first phase, that first signal for parents and teachers, that ought to be printed in women's magazines, for instance.

We concede education and scholarship their expertise. But we don't want to be left in complete ignorance. Moreover we also want *our* expertise to be recognised. After all, we know our child in a completely different way from the experts. We don't put a label on him, to us he is simply Enno. An individual with a unique combination of qualities; like every child, a case apart in fact.

In Enno's case, for instance, it is notable that in some things he is much further ahead than his contemporaries. That was always so. As a small child he wasn't interested in toy cars

— he never sat playing with them. But he was curious about how his father's car worked. He was always particularly interested in all kinds of things, especially if they had to do with insights and understanding. He is fascinated by things that have to do with thinking. But simply to learn something by heart unthinkingly...that means nothing at all to him.

We believe that a lot of people have a little of this and a little of that in their make-up. But in Enno's case it has been shared out wrongly. Or perhaps not wrongly but differently. That probably applies to other dyslexic children too. They are often good at things which the primary schools do not yet have such a need of. But we think that if their problems are catered for they can achieve a lot. That is something we have also experienced in our family. But how are you to help if in fact the schools are suffering from undercapacity and if even teachers at Remedial Schools do not know exactly what dyslexia implies?

The only thing we can come up with is to make our own limited contribution. To do that, as parents you have to be thoroughly daring and prepared to make an effort. And you must be creative, able to respond to what comes your way, as you can never actually say: this is the key to it all. With Enno we have always tried to give him — figuratively speaking — a tool-kit which he can use to put things together himself, as once he could reason something out he had made a big step forward. Hence we gave him rules of language and then it was hammer, hammer, hammer — but in as enjoyable a way as possible of course.

As parents we are convinced that to be able to support your child you need to keep following thoroughly what is going on at school: not only in relation to children with learning difficulties, of course, but it applies to them, perhaps, to a greater degree. Many parents go to a parents' evening and have a cup of coffee, and the head teacher's authority does the rest. But if you hear adults who are themselves dyslexic, they always say, 'I overcame it thanks to my parents'. By that they are referring primarily to the understanding and dedication which their parents showed. We are very well aware that that comes first. But in fact the exercises we did with Enno are also part of that.

Commentary by Specialists

THE OVERLAP BETWEEN SCHOOL AND HOME

The distinction that is made in our society between 'school' and 'home' is perhaps rather artificial, but it is a fact that in the course of time a certain allocation of tasks has grown up between the two involvements with children. But between these two worlds there is also a considerable overlap. This is precisely the area where parents can continue to put their stamp on their child's school career and, conversely, where teachers — voluntarily or involuntarily — have an influence on pupils' ups and downs at home. To start with the latter aspect: it is well known that dyslexic children take a considerable part of their school troubles home with them. They may not put their feelings directly into words, but for anybody with understanding it soon becomes clear if things are not going quite right at school. In fact, parents can become aware of it sooner than the teacher, who has to divide his or her attention among a large group of children. Moreover children tend to express themselves to their parents with fewer inhibitions than at school, where they have to conform to complex rules of social behaviour.

The first task reserved for parents as far as their child's school life is concerned is therefore to signal snags and problems. Where are things not running as they should? Of course, things must not stop at this signalling function. In the context of a good relationship with the school, solutions need to be found. This collaboration between parents and school is important to every child, but particularly for a child with learning problems. Where the two entities respect each other's knowledge and skill and recognise the reciprocal influences it must be possible for a constructive whole to grow.

Difficulties with the claims of the school as such lie in a completely different area of parental functioning. It is undeniable that to a large extent these occur in the territory of the teaching staff. We therefore often see things going wrong when the teacher, in the best relationship with the parents, gives 'little exercises' to take home, as such lessons are always a stumbling block for the pupil. They are not attainments he or she can proudly show his parents, but expressions of failure. And no child enjoys bringing them home. Concrete practising of weak learning achievements must therefore if at all possible not be done by the parents. It is hard to be dogmatic about this, incidentally, as parents are often forced to take refuge in such exercises when the school completely fails to recognise the dyslexic pupil's deficiencies. But in the area of reading and writing there is considerable overlap between the world of the home and the world of school. The home front should be able to stimulate the child in these areas, making him or her enthusiastic by being involved with him in a way that is not achievement-oriented. One thinks here of reading aloud or reading together, so that in spite of his failings at school the child continues to find pleasure in reading books. In addition repeating with the child things he or she has mastered is a good way of exercising without it being too threatening.

Of course numerous other enjoyable ways can be devised to combine the achievements at school with home life. For example, one thinks of keeping a diary together, or a log book on holiday. That at least demonstrates the usefulness of learning to write. Incidentally, in those circumstances it is more important that the child should learn to set down an idea on paper so that it can be read and understood rather than that the results should be completely free of mistakes. In short all those activities which have a stimulating effect on the child's attitude to problem areas lie pre-eminently in the parents' domain. In this their specific knowledge of the child and what he or she enjoys will be put to good use. Exercises oriented towards achievement are better left to others, to the specialists in that area. As with every rule, however, so there are exceptions to this one too. If, therefore, a plan of treatment is being drawn up, it is always important to set out in it what the parents' task is.

QUESTIONS

What should you do if you suspect that your child is dyslexic?

First — discuss the problem with the class-teacher and with the head. They will recommend further investigation from a schools' support service — which can have a variety of names, depending on the local education authority — or a session with an educational psychologist. If, after this, you are still not satisfied, then contact your nearest Dyslexia Institute — you will find the number in the telephone directory under Dyslexia.

If the school will not refer you to another agency, then contact your local education offices and ask them for the name and address of the Principal Educational Psychologist and explain the problem in a polite letter. You should be offered an appointment for your child with a psychologist at no charge. Alternatively, you will usually find a psychologist who will carry out independent testing listed under 'Psychologists' in the 'Yellow Pages' directory. Be sure to ask the amount of the fee you will have to pay before making an appointment. It can be very expensive.

To what extent does the advice of specialists take account of the special knowledge which parents have of their child?

Parents' special knowledge of their children is a necessary part of arriving at a proper diagnosis, as only the parents know the child's previous history; and describing and recording all the facts about the child's development, what is called 'anamnesis', is part of the diagnosis. This part is at least as important is undergoing various tests.

Then it is normal to consult with the parents about the dyslexic child; after all, they know best what will strike a chord with the child and what will not.

As parents how can one assess whether your child should have special teaching?

It may be possible to have lessons at the nearest Dyslexia Institute, or from a teacher recommended by them. There is a small number of independent schools which specialise in teaching dyslexic children. The fees are usually paid by parents but it may be possible in an extreme case to have your child made the subject of a 'Statement of Special Educational Needs' with the specialist school named as the appropriate placement for your child. In this case, the local education authority would be responsible for the fees but would review the placement on an annual basis.

How far can you leave it to the teacher to assess your child's learning attainments?

It is risky to leave assessment of learning attainments to the teacher alone. Only if the person concerned is a specialist in learning problems, in other words has both theoretical knowledge and practical experience in those areas, can it be supposed that he or she will be able to make an expert judgement. But only very exceptionally will teachers be able to fulfil those conditions. Ultimately a diagnostic test is always necessary in order to evaluate the problem and be able to draw up a plan of treatment.

Have teachers at Remedial Schools had special training?

In principle teachers at Remedial Schools have had the same teacher training as teachers at ordinary primary schools. Although many have done an additional course of one kind or another, it is as well to realise that to attend a course is not to be trained. After attending four evenings of lectures about dyslexia, teachers will undoubtedly know more about it, but it would nevertheless be difficult to regard them as experts in the field. Parents must therefore always remain alert concerning schools of this kind.

CHAPTER 5
Taking Charge

Does it Make Sense to have Expert Help for a Dyslexic Child?

Dyslexic children have a pronounced weakness in language. But is that something you just have to reconcile yourself to and try to make the best of? Or is there something you can do about it, and if so what?

Perhaps it is simply that dyslexic children need some extra time because they are slower. They lag quite a long way behind their contemporaries in reading and writing, but if you do not put too many difficulties in their way they will cope — although they will probably never become enthusiastic readers...

Or the other extreme: could dyslexia perhaps be overcome by doing certain specific exercises? Is it possible to adjust the unfair distribution of talents by means of training?

Hajo's parents are taking the middle way. They accept his handicap as a fact, but consider that expert assistance can help him to learn to live with it.

The Parents of Hajo (Aged 12) tell their Story

THE TEST

Hajo went through infants' school normally. At that time we did not notice anything special. The teacher rated him among the better pupils, at any rate from average to better. So at that stage there was no evidence at all of him falling behind.

On the contrary, because his birthday is in October he actually spent three years at infants' school and when he went to primary school he could already do sums up to 20, adding and subtracting. He enjoyed those enormously. Often they then start writing little words too, but what we did notice was that when they were busy on that he never joined in; he just wasn't interested in it at all.

Then he went into the first primary school class. The first report was excellent. But the second showed that from January Hajo had not kept up. He had got rather behind in reading and writing. The teacher then advised us to start doing some extra exercises with him at home, practising with him each evening and reading with him a little. And we did that constantly, until the summer holidays.

From that period we still remember one little incident which only began to take on more significance later. One evening we went upstairs to put him to bed and he really was a little upset. He simply kept asking: 'How do you write the word "giant" again?' And it was only three or four years later that he had had to stay behind with the teacher that day because he still couldn't write 'ia'. He had also practised it with us at home for a while and evidently he felt he simply couldn't do it. All the other children could and he felt it was out of his reach. So that was what had caused that flood of tears, a dreadful feeling of impotence. Hajo was able to go up from the first year to the second, but now he could hardly do his sums any more. If you said, 'What is 5 + 2?' the answer was '8?'. He was completely afraid. He was frightened that if he did sums he would do those wrong too. And so everything did go completely wrong. My father is a teacher himself and he said at the time that he had never experienced anything like it. He said: 'I can't understand him losing it. Surely once you can do something you can do it?'

The last two weeks of the holiday Hajo had to start again on little tasks, the teacher had said; then he could go up into the second class. When school had been back about three weeks we went to ask how things were going. The teacher said, 'I haven't noticed anything out of the ordinary, so I'm able to set the same work for everybody'. But before November we were again hearing things like 'Yes, there does seem to be something'. So more homework, every evening right after dinner, as you need to bring some regularity into it, otherwise the child gets completely disorientated.

Matters continued like that until after the Christmas holidays. Then if Hajo had to do an exercise at home he would become difficult, although he isn't actually a difficult child at all. He started to bang doors and cry — really dramatic outbursts. He simply wouldn't do it. And each week we would go bravely back to the school to collect exercises. But if he did do them, at school they were simply put on one side — there was no time to look at them. No attention was paid to them, to say, for instance: 'You've done that well, Hajo'. He was simply given a fresh pile of exercises.

The difficulty for Hajo was also that he did not see any results. He could work till he was blue in the face but it made absolutely no sense to him. He just couldn't keep up with the school. And everyone needs to progress. For instance, nobody will say: 'I've been learning to play the piano for five years now and I'm still not getting anywhere with it but I still enjoy it'. It just isn't like that.

Meanwhile there was an article about word-blindness in *Margriet* (a Dutch women's magazine). In addition we were phoned up by somebody who said: 'Watch *Here and Now* on television tonight'. We'd also started reading various items about it. We were genuinely searching. We didn't know that word 'dyslexia' then, but we knew I had it too. I used to have the same problems at school. At primary school I always failed the dictations. Then they said I had not practised properly and I had to write it out ten times. Eventually I said: 'There it is, it's already done' — because I had already written it out dozens of times whilst I'd been learning it.

So in Hajo I recognised myself: 'O dear, that's just how I was'. And then you want things to go more easily for your child than they did for you. That's why we told the school we wanted him to be tested. But Hajo was not eligible for the Schools Advisory Service. There were children in his class who were just that little bit worse than him. And they could only test one or two children in each class. Hajo was the third, I think, so he missed the boat.

Then we said to each other: 'Well, we *do* want him to be tested', and we went to a private organisation. That was in February when Hajo was in class two. He was tested by a remedial teacher, Paula. It was something he wanted too, as he thought: 'Then perhaps something will be done about it'. At ten o'clock he went off there and he was able to stay and have lunch there. After the introductory discussion we just went home and at about half past two we were telephoned to say we could go and collect him.

A report on the test was prepared for us, with a copy for the school. They would appreciate it, they said, if someone from the school would like to be present at the discussion of the report, as the question of what, if anything, ought to be done would then be considered. The school cooperated in doing that, albeit hesitantly. It turned out that Hajo was dyslexic. He was then about a year behind with his reading. Plurals such as 'mouse' becoming 'mice' he hadn't been able to get the hang of at all. He could only spell phonetically pure words. As soon as a difficulty arose he was in a complete fog. Round about March he was still at the level of class one.

We were told that the best thing would be to do certain specifically oriented exercises with him. 'But', Paula the remedial teacher said, 'that is not the parents' task, because as parents you have a completely different link with him. It is a school problem and must remain so. If you start to do exercises with him it will become a problem at home'.

So it was best that it should be done at school, under supervision. And as the teaching staff had no time to spare, we decided that Paula herself should do it.

COOPERATION WITH THE SCHOOL

The teacher would discuss at school how Hajo's remedial teaching could be tackled. A week later we went to the school. He had talked about it in the team and they had given their consent for it to take place in school time. But the extra lessons could not be given at the school, as that would create a difference, with one child getting them and another not. We were paying for the extra lessons and that would create an inequality.

Finally we decided that Hajo would have two three-quarter hour sessions a week at home. A start was then made, quite separately from the school. For the rest the school simply acted dumb. We got the impression that they felt that someone was poking about behind their backs, that they were afraid of having their knuckles rapped. They naturally start to feel unsure of themselves when you fetch someone in from outside. They start to think: Those parents have the impression that we're not capable of teaching Hajo to read and write properly, so they've brought somebody else in.

Another thing we kept coming across the whole time was that the teaching staff regarded the problems as all being caused by 'fear of failure'. And that fear of failure, they thought, resulted from us expecting too much from our child. Now certainly we do believe that Hajo had become afraid of failure right across the board, but in our view that was because of his language skills problems. Once Hajo was being helped by Paula with his language his arithmetic improved too, so as far as that was concerned we were in fact proved right.

So at the end of the second year we had a child who admittedly was poor at reading and dictation, but was good in other subjects. He was therefore able to go up. But we felt a certain amount of frustration at the school's not accepting that Paula was busy working with him, at the absence of cooperation with the teachers. Paula said: 'It is of great importance that I should be able to call in to see the teacher at the odd moment. It only needs to be five minutes, to say what I'm busy doing with Hajo'.

We also had the feeling that because of this we were not able to get the maximum return from the extra lessons. Because whilst what Paula was doing was very good, it did not link up with the school. She didn't do anything related to the things which were happening at school. Nor could she, as she was simply left in ignorance about them. She did ask Hajo on the odd occasion: 'Ask if you can bring this or that along'. But it was evidently too much work for the teacher to look into it, as nothing came of it.

He always had a good excuse, of course: 'I am so busy, with thirty children'. One can well imagine that. And he said to us: 'Hajo is getting those extra lessons because you're able to pay for them. But I know two or three who are even worse than Hajo. And what am I to do with them?' But Paula said: 'That's exactly it. I can perhaps offer that school something from which they too could benefit!'

Meanwhile she went to another school and there she did have contact with the teachers. They would say to her: 'I've got this problem or that problem. What would *you* do about it?' There was a certain amount of interaction, reciprocity. For one would think: you're busy teaching them all a particular subject. Yet your heart's in it. Our concern, of course, was with Hajo, but we always said: 'We hope lots more children will benefit too'.

Another point was that Paula is paid according to the parents' income. And if there is nothing else for it she works for nothing. So we said to the school: 'The parents of other children with problems simply need to get in touch with her. The money side will be taken care of'. Hajo didn't have to occupy such an exceptional position, as far as that went. But other parents simply didn't investigate the possibilities as we did, so little more was done for their children.

When Hajo went up from class two to class three we again asked: 'Can he be given extra teaching at school?' But still the answer was: 'No, we cannot make any special distinction'. Fortunately he had a very good teacher in class three. She was more interested in the problem than the teacher in class two had been. She also kept Paula *au fait* with what she was doing and the way in which she was presenting it. There was more intensive contact, and this enabled Paula more to match her way of working to the school's.

One day Paula said: 'Hajo cannot cope at all with those dictations at school. He simply can't manage them, they are far too difficult. He's doing dictations with me twice a week at his own level. He should give those dictations a miss, otherwise every time he'll be confronted by something he cannot do and that will be such a blow to him'. The class teacher went along with that tremendously well, giving the rest of the class dictations whilst Hajo worked on his at home with Paula.

But in the fourth year Hajo got a different teacher again, who was not interested at all. One day we went to see him, because Hajo was in floods of tears again. This was because that teacher didn't show so much consideration for him as the one in class three. With her he had caught up well and now it was going wrong again.

So we had continually to fight and be on the alert. Paula, for example, had said that Hajo was also troubled by problems of concentration. That seems to be part of the problem. She said: 'When he's sitting next to me he's always fiddling about and his eyes quite often wander when he's reading'. And because he is so quiet, a boy like that is put next to one of the biggest trouble-makers in the class! For quite a while he sat right next to this boy. Of course, nobody wants that for their child, but our problem was: Hajo would be affected by it from time to time. As a result he had significant sleeping problems during that period. Often he wouldn't fall asleep until around half past ten.

So in the fourth year we asked the teacher for a little understanding for this kind of thing. We didn't want Hajo to be put in an exceptional position, but we did want a little account to be taken of it.

But he simply wouldn't do it. For example, he said: 'Hajo must take part in the dictations, for the best thing is that he should know he can't do them'. He was also just that little bit hostile towards us, though fortunately not towards Hajo — we naturally kept an eye open for that. But I believe he thought we wanted to make Hajo into something special.

In class five we had the same teacher again. Meanwhile Paula continued to plug away: 'I will get through to that school'. Meanwhile there was some dislocation at school. The school was too crowded and three classes had to be moved a good distance away, to another school. One was Hajo's, which gave us an important argument for saying: 'Now the extra lessons *must* be given at school'. For he was simply too far away to be able to get home for the extra lessons. When we finally brought the matter to the school committee, which we had lobbied vigorously beforehand, in January we finally got the outcome we had wanted. After three years of knocking Hajo would get his extra lessons at school! As a result Paula was better able to respond to the way things were going at school, and the results were noticeable. He also acquired significantly more self-confidence. Now it really is only a school problem, it seems. And the nice thing is: now that Paula works at the school that teacher has also slowly come round somewhat. It seems that it is only now that he understands what we were up to all that time.

SO LONG AS THEY CAN REASON THINGS OUT

It does make a difference whether a child does exercises with his parents or with someone else. Because if as a parent you have to keep saying: 'You're doing this wrong, Hajo, do it again', the child will become angry. But he's never found that a problem with Paula. He has a very good relationship with her, a relationship of a very different type.

The most difficult aspect of practising with him, we found, was that you have no material for comparison. His classmates also made mistakes, of course, but if Hajo made a mistake, our hair immediately stood on end, because from him it was 'a problem'. Parents of a child which has no difficulties do not get worked up about a single mistake. They say, 'Now then, you've written that wrong'. And he'll say, 'Oh yes'. But with us something like that was a thunderclap, because we had become too fixated by that one problem. That's why it was good that Paula took over, also because as a remedial teacher she also applied a certain method and system for this type of child. So with Hajo she simply started to work at the level he had got stuck at in class one. Or perhaps even some way below it. At the start they cut and stuck lots of material; they laid out all manner of words. But because Hajo was still only in class two, that was possible.

There are also children, of course, who are only found to be dyslexic in class four, five or six. If they have to go back to the class-one level work, it doesn't succeed. By then they are too big for it. By then they have taught themselves so many things to shield themselves against it... Things that are not so easily unlearnt. So in our opinion it is very important that you latch on to it early. In that respect we were lucky with Hajo!

Paula proceeded like this: if he had to read, at first they continued for just as long as he read without error. And only later did they work to time. So usually it took three weeks to get through one piece of text. They also did dictations. First Paula said a sentence and Hajo had to repeat it after her to show that he had remembered it. Then he wrote it down, and then he read it back. So it was a matter of continually checking what he had done. But of course in class it is never done like that. There the children start to write even before the teacher has finished the sentence... As a result of all that practice the day came when understanding and reading started to go well again. You could tell that from the written problems in maths. But reading accurately was another matter. Whether he was reading 'stocking' or 'sock' didn't make all that much difference to him. And he still has problems with the articles. If it says 'de' he reads 'het' and vice versa.[1] He thus reads very superficially, not exactly what it says but the broad outlines.

Of course there are also things with dyslexia which cannot be practised. Those you just have to accept. For instance Paula says that Hajo has a very weak short-term memory. You can tell that from the fact that, for example, he doesn't know the names of his classmates, only those of his immediate friends. As his schooldays go by, the names of the other children gradually become fixed, of course. But that is a matter of long-term memory and that is good.

According to Paula there's nothing that can be done about his short-term memory handicap. You have to regard that as a given, you can't improve it by training. You can only try to get around the problem, just as in the case of blood vessels: if one gets blocked another takes over. A dyslexic person can only hope that he has access to such compensation mechanisms. And in Paula's opinion that is nearly always the case.

Hence dyslexic children can often do a great deal by means of rules. If they can reason it out they are already a big step forward. So Paula gave Hajo great big tables to take to school with him. Then he could see the rules when he was working. And the time came when they were so firmly fixed in his head that he no longer needed to have them on his desk. So if you simply have rules and time to apply those rules, the rest is often a matter of repetition, for ever repeating. It needs to be really engraved on the memory. The other subjects are now going really well and that is perhaps because Paula gets him to work in such a structured way. Because of her he is starting to think and work more methodically, paying more attention to rules now that he can evidently use them so well. And other children of that age still wander rather aimlessly on, just waiting for everything to fall into their lap. Most things at school, for instance, are simply offered. They are given, say, 25 words — a list of words. But as for why it's 'sit' with one 't' but 'sitting' with two, they are not told that. That's a question of practice, and then it's remembered.

The teacher who now has Hajo, in class six, asked whether perhaps Hajo could take his table of rules into school sometime. He had realised that the method they were now using needed supplementing, as there were far too many children who were having problems. This means that the other children can derive enjoyment from our having brought Paula in, as language problems can, of course, also arise to a certain extent from the method being used.

If they were presented with clearer rules at school both dyslexic children and the others would benefit. The question is, of course: to what extent have we done Hajo a service by involving him with these subjects in such a concentrated way? What would the outcome have been if we had not acted as we did? We think that things would have become impenetrable for him at school. He was for ever being given new things even when he had not absorbed the old ones. So to start with he needed more time. But at a Remedial School, in an atmosphere where he could have coped more calmly...? We don't know. At Remedial Schools, of course, there isn't an approach that is really oriented towards dyslexia. And a child of that age, who isn't given any special attention — there's a great deal that will pass him by. There will then be a number of aspects that are not picked up.

When I was his age I didn't receive any help either. But over time you start to read more, as you acquire interests and so on. The newspapers, for instance. When I write I still make lots of mistakes and often it is pure guesswork. I don't have so many little rules at my disposal as Hajo does. That's why I don't have any confidence at all in what I write down. All those methods give Hajo something to hold onto, of course. But because I didn't have any expert help, it's a bit like a quicksand for me. At any rate Hajo is pulling the strings himself now. He knows the spots where he can go wrong.

But the fact is he still has to be attentive. If he doesn't reflect about what he's doing he still makes mistakes. He always has to think, but the difference now is that he knows what he has to think about. And that's an important bonus. It is perhaps even the case that you don't always immediately see the results of that specialist help. But a child is given a structure which he can later fill out himself when he can cope with things more consciously. It will perhaps take years before that reaches full development.

As things stand now, we are already very satisfied. At the end of class five, as far as reading was concerned Hajo was at the level of the end of class three. And in spelling: Paula said that he probably won't be conspicuously behind in the bridging class.* He has caught up reasonably well in that area. The spelling is therefore going better than reading. Paula says: 'That is a common pattern with dyslexia. With expert help you often see precisely that development'.

LEARNING TO LIVE WITH IT

As things were in class two, if we had not then been helped things would probably have gone completely awry. He was also acquiring other problems. Behaviour problems. He was starting to fail in areas like arithmetic. Had things continued like that he would certainly not have gone up to the next class. He would perhaps have had to go to a Remedial School and again that would have cost the local authority a lot of money.

And all that whilst in fact he is a very normal child. With that help he can get through primary school quite straightforwardly. He has kept his friends in the neighbourhood. He belongs with them, they have accepted what is special about him. And since Paula has come to the school he too has completely accepted it. It is now an isolated problem, and is no longer so all-embracing. It is just these language skills. In addition to those he has his football, arithmetic... We have Paula to thank for all this. She has supported him tremendously well. And the emotional side of it is an aspect in itself. With Paula he could do it. In class two he got picture cards from her, or a sticker: 'Well done again!' At his own level he always achieved well with her, and so he got the idea that he really could do it. At school he wasn't yet succeeding, as there he had fallen behind. He was struggling there, going slower and slower and getting more and more behind. But with Paula he progressed. It was clearly noticeable. When she gave him tests, she compared them with the previous ones. He then managed a specific score, say 43, and six months later it would be 47. Once she had to cheat, when there had been no change. She said he had scored one more, because then at least Hajo had the idea that he was making progress. From that she was also able to see that she had evidently increased the difficulties too fast in that period, so she went back to a rather more leisurely pace, as it is very important that a child in this situation should see results. It mustn't seem like a mountain which makes him think: 'I'll never get to the top'.

So Hajo was indeed progressing, but slowly. Enormous patience was needed and you had to take care that you never discouraged him. Paula always did other things with him in which he was able to succeed a little. What was most striking in the early days was therefore not the results. In spite of the expert help, they were not so great, especially when as parents you could see that the simplest things, which he really ought to have been able to do, were still going completely wrong...

No, the most positive aspect was the confidence which Hajo regained in himself. His arithmetic improved. All his angry tears and frustration were gone completely and gave us no further problems. And that is terribly important. The problem mustn't be allowed to get to where it actually isn't.

Thanks to the help he was being given Hajo was at least no longer afraid of failing. And because he has always talked about it openly he accepts his problem for what it is. He knows he is bad at language skills. If he has to read out loud in class, he sometimes hears the others sighing around him. Then they say, 'Oh, it's Hajo's turn. Can't we go on to the next in line?' But all the same Hajo does read. Then the whole class simply has to go more slowly. And for that you have to be very sure of your ground!

We are lucky that Hajo is now getting on well. All the factors have worked in our favour. The fact that we latched onto the problem early, for example. And that Hajo has such a good bond with Paula. Because that is also important, *who* it is that helps you. Then in addition the child must have the attitude of wanting to work on the problem. And if emotional problems have arisen which are so great that the child no longer has that will, you first need to work on those.

If you were now to ask us what we think the most important thing about the specialist help is, then we would unhesitatingly say: 'The emotional aspect'. Naturally, Hajo has progressed technically, and we are very glad about that. But in addition the big advantage is that he is being tremendously supported in his handicap. He is being, as it were, coached in it, you could say. He is learning to live with it. If you set those two aspects side by side, then we would say: 'The technical aspect is less important than the emotional one'. That is why we think that other ways of paying attention to the handicap are also useful, at any rate for that aspect of the matter. For by means of those a child needs to be able to cope with the whole of the rest of his life. And language skills, well, they are above all a question of communication. So long as you can make yourself clear, surely those mistakes don't make such a lot of difference?

Commentary by Specialists

THERE IS NO STANDARD TREATMENT

Dyslexia is not backwardness in development which can be corrected by giving a child more time or by arranging for him or her to do more of the same exercises. If it is suspected that a child is dyslexic, it is not sensible just to wait, as matters will not rectify themselves of their own accord. Nor, on the other hand, should one immediately expect miracles from a particular approach to treatment.

Dyslexia arises from the faulty processing of language information. This processing can be trained, of course, but it will remain a weakness, especially as during a child's school life fresh reliance is repeatedly placed on it. Scarcely will a dyslexic child have partly overcome the obstacles to learning to read and write words that contain pure sounds than they will encounter words for which you need a rule to decide how they should be written. And as soon as this is under their belt they will be faced with the foreign words that have entered the mother tongue. Once these difficulties are overcome, it starts all over again in the form of a different language. Certainly now that subjects such as foreign languages are being introduced as early as primary school, dyslexic children are coming under great and continuing pressure. This means they need continuing assistance, which can help them to cross many of these thresholds. As we have already said, this assistance does not remove the problem, but can considerably alleviate it. To bring this about, an individual approach is to be preferred, as it can then be matched precisely to the strengths and weaknesses of the child concerned. As a rule these strengths and weaknesses will come to light via a prior psychological diagnostic test and subsequently be elaborated in a plan of treatment. Thereafter the child's progress will be assessed regularly, to enable the help to be adjusted as appropriate.

In general treatment will be concentrated on three different areas. These are, firstly, a general training in language or linguistic requirements, where the child evidently falls short in that area. Then reading and spelling themselves are systematically put under the microscope and, thirdly, attention is paid to improving the often weak concentration of dyslexic children and reinforcing their motivation to take part in the remedial programme.

In this way ample practice and long-term help often make it possible to effect remarkable improvements in reading and writing.

QUESTIONS

Is it possible to treat and help dyslexia at any age?

Treating dyslexia consists of teaching the system of 'reading' and/or the system of 'writing', and this is possible at any age. But the same applies as in other contexts: the older someone is the more difficult it is in general to learn something new. But perhaps the hardest thing of all is to unlearn old habits so that new ones can take their place. Hardly anyone will first come into contact with reading and spelling when they are older. That means that a great number of mistakes will have crept into earlier attempts to gain mastery of these systems. A not inconsiderable amount of work has to be done if such mistakes are to be eliminated. Against that, however, people wanting to start to tackle the problem at a later stage in life are often highly motivated. More than their younger counterparts, they can see how useful reading and writing are and therefore know how to apply what they have learnt in a more meaningful way.

Can dyslexia be corrected by improving motor skills?

Dyslexia does not result from poor motor skills, though of course poor motor skills can accompany dyslexia. In particular the minor motor skills of dyslexic children by no means always function optimally. This is manifested in cramped penmanship and notably poor handwriting. For children in whom this combination occurs it therefore makes sense to provide training for both the dyslexia and the poor handwriting; exercising motor skills in the hope of improving reading and spelling, however, is a waste of time.

In general do Remedial Schools prepare a special plan of treatment for a child?

In England and Wales, all children who have a 'statement' issued under the 1981 Education Act should have their special needs itemised in general terms. Individualised programmes are not normally provided. The 1988 Education Reform Act gives every child attending schools in the state system the right of access to a National Curriculum. Children's progress is assessed regularly and these assessments may lead to more individualised programmes being developed.

What is the difference between a remedial teacher and a remedial educationalist?

There are no formal requirements beyond initial teacher-training for teachers in the United Kingdom except those working with the deaf or the blind. In practice, many teachers working with remedial groups, support services or Remedial Schools, have undertaken further qualifications in this speciality. These vary from short practical courses to diplomas or master's degrees taken at polytechnics or universities.

NOTE TO CHAPTER 5

1. 'De' and 'het' are the singular definite articles in Dutch, for common and neuter nouns.

CHAPTER 6

Not Popular

Is Dyslexia also a Social Problem?

Is dyslexia limited to halting reading and shaky writing? Or does it perhaps also affect the way children get on with their contemporaries?

One can assume the latter. Children do not like being exceptions. They prefer to live in a large uniform whole. Anyone who stands out needs to be very sure of his ground in children's culture if he is not immediately to be excluded. That is why as a child you try as far as possible to adapt to the expectations of your age group. And if you think you are not meeting those expectations in all respects, you will perhaps try to camouflage your deficiencies or compensate for them in some other way.

'But', relates Bart in the narrative that now follows, 'other children have an unerring knack of seeing through that'.

Another aspect of dyslexia which can affect social functioning is the fact that dyslexic children often find themselves at a school which in certain respects is too easy for them. And children feel that. They feel they are elevated far above their classmates. They do not belong there. One can well imagine that these feelings will affect their behaviour, which in turn does not make it any more acceptable to the other children. This and other consequences of dyslexia in areas where the problem doesn't actually belong are discussed in this chapter. These effects can perhaps not wholly be prevented, but they are well worth pondering.

Bart (Aged 17) tells his Story

I AM DIFFERENT

When I was one or two years old — at any rate so my mother has told me — I cried a tremendous amount. I demanded lots of attention and was regarded as troublesome, not to put it any higher than that. Stacks of psychological reports were written about me but none of them really helped. Things went rather better, I think, when my mother started to adopt a rather more strict approach towards me, when she started ignoring me more when I played up.

At infants' school there were no problems, at any rate I haven't heard of any. But things started to go wrong in the first primary school class. By Christmas most of the children could read a good number of words, but I couldn't. I remember how the other children always had to help me. All the same, at the end of that year I went up to class two with them in the normal way.

Then I realised that in some way or another the other children didn't like me very much. I can still remember how the teacher used to have to intervene to get things done for me. If I wanted to borrow felt-tipped pens or something like that from one of the other children the answer was always no. Looking back, I think I wasn't popular because I was always boasting about all the things I could do. Grown-ups find that amusing and laugh at it, as if to say: 'There's no harm in it'. But other children come down on it like a ton of bricks.

In class two I had a fantastically nice teacher who was willing to try anything, but absolutely nothing worked. Also there were 34 children in the class, so she couldn't spend so much time on me. After advice from a psychology practice I then found myself at a Remedial School at the other end of town. It was presumed that I would more easily be able to work at my own pace there. The word 'dyslexia' was never mentioned then. I had a 'learning problem'. I was going there because I still couldn't read. I remember telling everybody I was going to the Remedial School because I had a damaged brain. That was at least comprehensible; they listened to that and also it was an interesting thing to have. For the first year and a half I felt tremendously comfortable at that school. And the year after that my reading began to come on somewhat; I was then perhaps at the level normally achieved after the first term at primary school. But at that point things stood still for a year, as the social problems then started to play a role. In the class with me there were a number of awful children. Hard to educate, antisocial, rejected by their parents and society. A lot from the children's home, for instance. And they tormented and hit me regularly. The teacher of that class didn't do anything about it, I think he thought I was a bit crazy.

I left there at Easter, as I was coming home in tears every day. It was an absolute disaster! Fortunately there was another Remedial School in the town and I then started going there. I was nine, I think. They didn't say I was dyslexic either, but they did help me. In the care of an ordinary teacher and a remedial teacher I was really crammed out. True, I was still tormented by the other children from time to time, but I was able to cope with it better by then. It no longer kept me lying awake at night. I enjoyed being at that school. I learnt a tremendous amount to my way of thinking. We worked like dogs; every day I had three quarters of an hour's homework to do, for instance. In addition I worked at home with my mother as well. She helped me with my spelling and we did dictations and things like that. Thinking back on it now, I realise I was fantastically lucky to have a mother like that, otherwise I wouldn't have got my school-leaving certificate yet. At the time, of course, I didn't think it was all that great to be working with her, though actually it was also a form of attention. And evidently I had a great need of that from way back. Attention and recognition.

The result was that until I was fourteen or fifteen I had all the attention I could want. My brother was a very calm child and also he got on well at school. He was very easy to get along with. Then people would say: 'He's such a delightful child'. I often found that difficult. It's one of the reasons why I still don't get on with him very well, I think. We were for ever quarrelling. We're also very different from each other. I always used to want to be just like my brother, as then I would be done with all the nagging.

When I went to secondary school my mother went to talk to them and asked for a policy plan for me. Right from the start I went there with the 'dyslexic' label, which I had even at that early stage. The school was a Montessori one, the only school that would accept that sort of problem. At any rate, that is what they claimed. But I realised early on that they were following no policy at all towards me. One teacher would have an understanding of the situation and another would not. Cooperation between the teachers on that score was really pathetic.

So there I was at that school. The year was divided into three terms and to my way of thinking the first term of that year went really badly. I would often burst into tears because I just couldn't cope. Then my mother pulled me through the first term, hauled me through the second and dragged me through the third. And then I went into the second class and that was a real revelation, as all of a sudden I could get on with the rest of the class!

All the same, I felt the whole time that I was really far above the other children. Perhaps it isn't really such a good feeling to have, and I can't actually explain what I mean by it. You could say that my general development was simply much greater. And that meant I didn't feel in the least settled at that school.

Now perhaps if I had carried on working hard I might have got to the Montessori grammar school. I would undoubtedly have been more at home there. But I didn't do very much work and when I went up it was only by a whisker. I was put into 3c, the slow stream, in which you spend five years working for your MAVO.* But that year too my motivation left a lot to be desired. For me school was a necessary evil. Then when I was in the third year we got a computer at home. At first I wasn't allowed to go near it but later I learnt how to get on with it. My handwriting is very hard to read but on that thing I could more easily read back what I had typed. Also, making corrections was as easy as pie, so I started doing more and more work on the word processor. At school they didn't really agree with it, but they accepted it.

So last year I went into 4c and by then I was doing nearly all my homework on the computer. It was only that machine that really taught me to read and write. It was as if I was starting to wake up after a long winter's sleep. For example I started reading the newspaper. I became more interested in all kinds of things. The subjects at school appealed to me more. History fascinated me greatly and for the first time I also started to show an interest in chemistry and physics. With reading it's like this: if a book grips me I read it to the end. I made enormous strides with word recognition.

It's the 'ai' sounds I'm still not very good at. And things like 'ea' and 'ee'. But I'm clear now about the how and why of double consonants. So things are going better now. A number of people say: 'You'll be faced with your reading and writing problems all your life'. But in a recent dictation I only had seven mistakes. That figure used to be of the order of twenty to thirty. But then you still only get a 3 for it...

It's true that spelling will never go automatically for me. If I want to write something down properly, I always have to think about it. Every word. And if I start to pay less attention my spelling is still a real disaster. That's terrible. But making corrections now goes better for me: I can find my mistakes. And so with the help of the computer I'm often able to produce very acceptable essays or close readings. Something else I have: I'm very good at retaining what I am told. If I have not prepared a chemistry test I still get an 8 or 9 with ease, as I've paid attention in class. The only thing is: I don't read carefully. So in a chemistry test I don't read the questions properly. That's my handicap. I can see that now, whereas I never used to be able to. Now I pay attention, reading questions twice for instance. Or I take the question over into the answer so that the master can see whether I've picked it up properly.

In maths, chemistry and physics I was on the wrong side of average in the class for four years. And now I'm one of the best. That's happened, I think, because I'm interested now. What's in there comes out, and so I'm also enjoying school.

My final exams are going very well. I think I am one of the
lucky cases.

DYSLEXIC CHILDREN ARE REALLY VERY NICE!

The worst thing, I used to find, was that I didn't have any
friends. When I think back to that time, I would lie in bed listening to the radio or watching anything and everything on TV.
I wouldn't be at all surprised to discover that this is a problem
that occurs with other dyslexic children. Of course, in principle
such children do not differ from other children, but all the same
in a certain way they are different. They often achieve less than
they could do on the basis of their intelligence. For that reason
they are put into schools where their interest is not specifically
encouraged. They don't feel at their ease there and so they find
it harder to make contact. Also they perhaps have a tendency —
at least, this is something I have noticed in myself — to be terribly conceited in class. They know absolutely everything better
than anyone else.

You can well imagine that they're not nice pupils at all,
either for the teacher or for the other children. And then to cap
it all, they're supposed to make allowances for someone like
that! It is really a difficult point, you see. Because once you
penetrate that, they can be really nice children, of course. It's
simply that they have to compensate for something.

I myself have now learnt to give up all that bragging, but it
was not until very late on that I cottoned on to it. That was when
a few boys said to me: 'You really must stop doing that. It's so
irritating'. Then I realised that you're also accepted just as you
are. I no longer pretend to be somebody else. Now I have friends
as well, just from the last year. Real friends: people for whom I'd
go through fire for and so would they for me. I've also thought:
if you're aiming to motivate dyslexic children you must perhaps
praise them in a slightly exaggerated way for the things they can
in fact do. Because from my own experience I know that with a
handicap like this you often have the feeling: 'What's the use of
it all?' You don't have any friends, you don't signify, either at

school or outside. That makes it really great to have something you are genuinely good at.

For instance, I've skated for many years and I was reasonably good at it. On the skating rink I was really something. I've taken part in the Dutch championships and that sort of thing. I really had something to latch onto there. In that way you're not confronted by just the problems. Now, in fact, I don't actually need the skating so much. I've been letting it run down a little.

The skating season starts in October and finishes in March. In that period you're really on the go early in the day, so you would think: school will have to play second fiddle to an extent. But the crazy thing is: those periods were always my best periods at school. I've noticed that the clockwork regularity of full days forces you to keep a certain discipline. But if you pass your time hanging around in front of the TV you get absolutely nothing done. I therefore like to divide up my time strictly. I plan everything to the last minute and that is a very satisfying experience.

But these are all insights which have come later. Until recently I've never really felt myself at ease when I've been at school and I regard that mainly as a social problem. You see, at parties I've met people from the grammar school from time to time and I feel a lot more at ease with them. We have more interests in common.

The problem parents of dyslexic children therefore face is the following choice. On the one hand: if I send him to an ordinary primary school he'll be banging his head against a brick wall. But at least he'll have girls and boys to be friends with. And on the other hand if I send him to a remedial school and later to the LBO* or the MAVO — in any event some way below his level — then he won't need to feel frustrated. But then the social aspects are so difficult.

I think a great many difficulties could be solved with a little understanding and extra help on the part of the school. Dyslexic children really ought to take a stand and demand that. We must demand from the schools that they should accept our problems and that consideration should be given to us in certain areas. More time, a different system of awarding marks, clear language rules (because at the moment it is a load of non-sense!), oral sessions and a lot of things distributed as hand-outs. But for people who are not familiar with it dyslexia is quite unimaginable, you see. Impossible to understand. That's why, for instance, there are still people who think what I have is an emotional problem, that I can't manage my feelings and that's why I transpose d's and t's. A very selective emotional problem, as it doesn't seem to have any effect on the exact subjects! It's only now that those subjects are working out, now that I have found my feet a little. At school I believe they think: 'It's a good job we kept Bart here!'

Commentary by Specialists

DYSLEXIC CHILDREN ALSO HAVE THEIR STRENGTHS

The most characteristic aspects of dyslexic children are their weaknesses. That is how they are classified. A child is dyslexic: that means he or she is bad at reading and writing. But we must never forget that a dyslexic child is always more than dyslexic. The dyslexia does not leave its mark everywhere and the trick is to ensure that the problem does in fact remain confined to the area where it belongs: reading and writing.

That is why it is a good thing to bring out those facets of a child which have nothing — absolutely nothing — to do with the dyslexia. This is no easy task, because if you have a 'problem child' it is often difficult not to put that problem in the centre of the stage and devote all one's attention to it.

It is also undeniable that a problem of that kind does demand lots of attention. And then also to have to expend energy on aspects that are, in fact, going well, which seem to go under their own steam — it's no easy challenge. But it is necessary. Dyslexic children must experience that in most areas they can get along perfectly well. In sport, for instance, or in arithmetic, maths and handicrafts. In those areas you cannot tell that a dyslexic child is actually dyslexic. It is therefore important that children should be able to take part in activities of that kind and be able to function normally out of school, without being an exception.

It is possible that a dyslexic child will even have very considerable strengths. This needs qualifying, as apart from the dyslexia a child will often be a very normally gifted individual. Nevertheless amongst dyslexic children there are others who develop special gifts in certain areas. Thus they often have a remarkable visual memory and evidence great spatial understanding. This can often be noticed very early on, when as toddlers they get hold of building toys. And if their talents in that direction do not become submerged by the problems of dyslexia, we later find that such children become photographers, engineers, carpenters, computer specialists, dentists or sculptors. From the fact that their relative aptitudes in these areas become apparent so early we can perhaps deduce that what one has here is not just a compensation mechanism for those aspects that do not go well. Such compensation can also play a part, of course, but in principle we are entitled to assume that against his innate weaknesses a dyslexic child can also juxtapose innate strengths. In contrast to an average child, whose verbal and visual capacities often do not diverge so greatly from each other, in the dyslexic child a language 'depression' and a spatial 'bump' are often found together in the aptitude profile. Incidentally it often happens that dyslexic people achieve high scores in listening tests and are thus aurally gifted and even perhaps musical.

Knowing this, we can ask ourselves whether dyslexia should still be regarded as a 'handicap', as what we are dealing with are children of a completely different type, a 'unilaterally gifted' type, one could say. Yet both parents and children themselves often experience this unbalanced range of aptitudes as a handicap. The cause of this lies not in the distribution of talents but in the way in which our society handles it. Most schools, for example, are designed for the standard child who achieves equally well in all subjects. Places can also be found for children who are bad in all subjects or good in all of them, even though they too have their own very specific difficulties. But children who on the one hand have difficulty functioning in the language area and on the other show reasonable or very good achievement in subjects such as mathematics — they just do not fit in. The school system has difficulty in accepting them. The problem is then either totally ignored, or generalised to other areas. It is either: 'The child has no problems whatsoever. He is sufficiently intelligent. You are expecting too much from him'. Or: 'She is stupid, unwilling, lazy and lacking in concentration'. Those are the two ways in which a school which is oriented towards the average child can respond. And neither reaction is appropriate to a dyslexic child's specific problems. Of course the child at school also feels that he or she doesn't fit in. One can readily understand that that is likely to have social consequences, and one therefore often sees dyslexic children withdrawing, so as to become as inconspicuous as possible, or starting to show tough, aggressive and boastful behaviour. To avoid things getting out of hand it is therefore necessary to cultivate an understanding at the school for the child's specifically weak, but also the strong, sides, and on the other hand to allow the opportunity outside school to be not a problem child but perhaps even a 'hot shot' at something.

QUESTIONS

Does the distance to the Remedial Schools where dyslexic children sometimes land up form an insuperable objection for many of those children?

By being placed in a different school children are often withdrawn from their normal 'street life', as their school friends generally live some way out of the neighbourhood. It is possible to cope with this problem, however, with a little cautious help on the part of the parents. For example, organise a little party some time, to which the neighbourhood children are also invited. Let the child take part in neighbourhood activities, or enrol him or her at a sports club, with the one purpose, of course — without the point being emphasised too much — of making friends around and about. It sometimes takes a little time before a chord is struck here.

Are most children at Remedial Schools antisocial?

Special schools have names which indicate what kinds of children they are for. Thus Remedial Schools are for children with learning and educational difficulties. What do these 'educational difficulties' imply? In general there are two types. First there are the more withdrawn, unsure children who have a fear of failure, who because of their problem have come to doubt their own capacities and as a result have become rather quiet and anxious. On the other hand there are the children who are very busy, mobile, over-active and rather tough and swaggering. With their over-rapid reactions, of course, these children are more conspicuous than the quiet children.

If this second type predominates, the result can be that the atmosphere in the school will take on a slightly aggressive character. This puts extra demands on the teaching expertise of the team. Incidentally, for children who manifest these problems too markedly and thereby exhibit antisocial behaviour, there is the ZMOK-school* where the school team is better equipped to cope with such children.

CHAPTER 7

From Pillar to Post

Are Things Always so Clear?

In the course of the previous chapters it will have become clear that dyslexia is a form of reading and spelling problem which in different children manifests itself to different degrees and at different times — but nevertheless: reading and writing are always the main constituents of the story. Clearly subordinate to that we have also encountered phenomena such as 'fear of failure' and problems making friends. But are things always so very clear?

The following story by a mother of four children, who all have to struggle to a greater or lesser extent with school problems, shows that there are sometimes many other aspects also involved. A child's temperament, for example. He or she can react so violently to failure as to make it virtually impossible any longer to determine the reason for the reaction. But the converse can also happen: a child can fail at school because of their struggle with serious psychological and emotional problems. In the first case we may be faced with a dyslexic child, whilst in the second according to the books there is no evidence of that. Either way, there will be implications for the way in which the child should be dealt with. How, then, do you unravel the confusing tangle of learning disturbances and emotional problems? It would seem to be an almost impossible task! In these cases, perhaps the best thing you can do as parents is to go by your feelings and do what seems best. But what if your feelings are diametrically opposed to the advice drummed into us by professional educators? Then, of course, things become even less clear. Our feelings are an uncertain master and they can often be outdone by arguments. All that then remains is perhaps a feeling of guilt.

But can you ever do things properly? Is there one correct road as regards coping with children? Although the advice of educational specialists sometimes suggests that there is, we ought perhaps to leave a question mark.

The choices which you make for your children are probably of much less importance than the love and understanding you can bring to them.

The Mother of Kees (Aged 18), Kim (Aged 16), Jeroen (Aged 9) and Marieke (Aged 8) tells her Story

KEES

It actually started when Kees was two. I remember how I was standing in the kitchen and he said something to me which I didn't understand. Then he became so terribly angry and kicked me wherever he could. And when I walked away he chased after me. He was already terrifically demanding and at a certain stage I consulted the Child and Family Guidance Clinic, who gave some advice on upbringing and so on.

As a toddler he was very small, he really was a toddler of a toddler. Then when he was six I thought to myself: Does that child really have to go to primary school? He was by far the smallest one in the class! So I went to the teacher and said: 'Wouldn't it be better if he stayed on at infants' school for another year?' She thought it was a ridiculous idea. 'He's such an intelligent child and he has such a big vocabulary and he's so good at this and so clever at that..'. Well, as a mother you're bound to feel a little flattered, now that I look back on it. And you think: No doubt she has a better insight than I do. The thing that both he and later Jeroen had difficulty with at that age was naming the colours. If I said: 'Pick up that red block', they would pick it up without hesitation. But if I then asked: 'What colour is that?' they could not remember what it was. And I would think: Surely you can't go to primary school if you don't know the colours?

But all well and good, the infants' school teacher persisted and so Kees found himself in the first primary class. And it was then soon evident that he wasn't really ready for school. For instance if he had to write 'book' and 'cook' he made the o's into splendid faces and that's as far as he got. The teacher was very often cross with him because he wasn't doing any work.

She told me that he sometimes deliberately broke the point of his pencil ten times a day. Then he could sharpen it again and then he would simply carry on drawing. There was no end result at all. Often he was given what he had written to bring home with him so he could finish it off there. That meant an hour crying at the kitchen table. When I saw that I often thought to myself: Oh, you poor boy, you're just an infants' school child still. You're simply not up to this!

The day came when I went to the teacher and said: 'In no way do I want Kees to be given work to bring home. If he can't manage it at school, let him just sit there'. But she said: 'Do you realise that he is really a very intelligent child? It's your fault if your child fails!' I can tell you, you then start to feel so unsure of yourself! I thought: Perhaps I'm doing it all wrong.

I'd actually been intending to take him away from school, but they said: 'Then you'll make it far too easy for him. It doesn't make sense to run away as soon as there's something you can't do well'. That was an argument which I was sensitive to, of course.

So in that class quite a strict approach was taken to Kees. This created great difficulty for me, because with me no longer allowing him to be given any homework they took other steps. For instance he was no longer allowed to do any gym — he had to finish off his work, or else he wasn't allowed to go outside at playtime. And if I then came to collect him at midday there was absolutely nothing I could do with him. I sometimes had nine children in the car, as to an extent we parents had divided the collection of the children up amongst us, but eventually Kees made this impossible. He was so aggressive when he came out of school that he would hit and kick all the other children; the mothers complained about it as well.

At home he was unmanageable. He terrorised his little brother if I turned my back for a moment. So in December I went back to the Guidance Clinic. Kees was then six and a half. He was tested, but I never had a report on the test, though it was discussed with me. They said: 'He is a particularly intelligent boy and there is nothing wrong with him. No learning abnormality, although it's still very early to be able to detect that'. But they did in fact find that he was as yet by no means ready for school. It would have been better if he had been at a more flexible school. I was then advised to put him into a Montessori school.

Well, in retrospect that was very bad advice. For what did they do at that Montessori school — for which in the first instance I was very grateful? They simply let the child draw. Because he had really got himself into problems at the other school they said: 'He's just not yet up to coping with language'. But what they did not do was tackle the problem of how to teach him. When Kees was in class four he was still busy doing class one lessons.

I tackled the school about it, of course, but I was simply not listened to. They said things like: 'Oh, he's intelligent enough and you're trying to stick a label on him. If it isn't going smoothly that's your fault for expecting a lot more from him than he can do'. Then I said: 'But the child cannot read at all. Surely there must be something wrong somewhere? If he's a child of normal intelligence there's surely something up?' But for all that they just thought I was being ambitious.

Psychologically, however, Kees had a fine time there at the Montessori school. He had close friends and there were always girls in love with him. He was in clover there. He would often do big drawings on all kinds of biological subjects and would sit for hours in the library examining biology pictures. But he didn't work through any proper programme.

Of course we tried to help him catch up with extra lessons and suchlike. In class five he had some extra lessons from the teacher, but I don't think they helped him much. If the basic knowledge is not there, everything is a quicksand. With a child like that you have to take a very fundamental approach, I think.

I discovered that when he was in class five and I tried to instil the two-letter vowels into him, the 'ai', the 'ou', the 'ea' and so on. These gave him tremendous difficulty. But thanks to a method I'd heard of, devised by a speech therapist, I finally drummed them into him.

In this way Kees finally reached class one of the HAVO*, albeit on a very precarious basis. There, for instance, he turned out not to know the months of the year, and all sorts of perfectly ordinary Dutch words, such as 'breakfast'. For a while he had extra teaching from a friend of mine, and all the time he was at the HAVO he was only able to do geography and history, because she read that out. He couldn't read fast enough to get through the work in an evening, you see. You would surely say to yourself: 'There's got to be something wrong with a boy like that'.

I'd come across the word dyslexia now and again at the Guidance Clinic. I'm also dyslexic, you see, so I didn't find that such a big mental leap. But they really don't like it, you know, if *you* come up with it. At any rate they assured me that Kees could not be dyslexic, as he wasn't having any trouble with left and right transposition. They kept insisting that there was absolutely nothing wrong with him.

Well, there he was at the HAVO, this 'superintelligent boy' with whom there was supposedly nothing wrong, spending ten hours swotting for an English test...and he got 2 out of 10 for it. I worked very intensively with him in the bridging class — I don't think I'd ever be able to do anything like that again — but it achieved nothing. Finally, at my wits' end, I put him into the junior technical school. There he got a 'c' in his junior technical diploma and he's now at the intermediate technical school.

Kees had tremendous difficulties at the junior technical school. It is perhaps a funny thing to say, but he became a completely different kind of boy, very gentle, not liking football and so on. But he *is* of a technical turn of mind. He is enormously adept and has terrific insight. Mechanical things are no problem. He also often sees solutions which are different from what others come up with. He enjoys making model aircraft or playing with the computer. So as far as that goes he's at home at technical school. But in another respect... Since he's left the HAVO he hasn't had any friends any more.

At intermediate technical school too he's had difficulties all along the line. All the subjects are going badly, yet I have the impression that his aptitude is greatest for the exact subjects. Reading is also involved, of course, but all the same I would have said he ought to be reasonably good at those subjects. But it is as if he has become more and more stupid over the years. It seems as if he has fallen asleep. He forgets everything all the time and often day-dreams.

He won't accept any help with his work from outside. I have the feeling that this is because he doesn't actually accept his handicap. And the result is that recently he has been really depressed. I simply don't know what to do next.

KIM

My second son is a hypersensitive child, though he can sometimes show a really aggressive side. With him too the problems started when he was still only two or three years old. When he was a toddler I often couldn't get him to sleep at all. He had dreadful nightmares. People said to me: 'What that child needs is a box on the ears now and again, as he's just putting all that on'. But I didn't at all feel he was making a fool of me, because after one of those nights he could often not remember anything of what had happened.

Later he suffered from great fears. He was afraid of death, and so on. He is still receiving psychiatric help for that. And I'm bound to say I've just no idea where that's all come from. I often think: Probably it's my fault. But all I know is that I've always been extremely fond of him and that I've been really loving towards him. As far as possible I've done what I thought was best. We have a good relationship, and I have an excellent bond with him.

When Kim came to the end of infants' school the teachers there said he wasn't ready for school proper. I was glad they were now saying this of their own accord, as when I had said the same thing about Kees two years earlier I had been met with a wall of indignation. But Kim's bad luck was that there was a complete change-round of staff at that infants' school and the teacher wasn't suitable for him. So we decided simply to send him to primary school and there let him work like a pre-school child at the start.

He went straight to the Montessori school, where his brother Kees had meanwhile also gone. And things went well, except that when he had reached class two he asked one day if he could join in the reading and writing lessons and they said: 'You're not up to that yet, Kim'. When later I asked: 'Is it really not possible for him to do any exercises in language yet? He himself does want to do some', back came the answer: 'We don't think he is far enough forward for them yet'.

So at the end of class three he was still messing about with language exercises from the beginning of class one. Then you think: 'It's all right them waiting for this famous "sensitive period", but it hasn't come. And I don't think you can wait and wait for ever'.

All the same to my way of thinking things went well at that time. It might seem as if one was taking the easy way out, but there were few obvious problems. I had a job for twenty hours a week, took the children to school in the mornings in my old 2CV, and there they stayed. That was normal there. On Wednesdays I used to get off earlier and so I was there at mid-day to collect them.

Kees became less aggressive at that Montessori school and Kim was still having nightmares, but otherwise things went along fine. But because I often used to sit up until one in the morning with Kim because of his nightmares, once again I went back to the Child and Family Guidance Clinic. There they looked at him and then they said: 'Are you actually aware that his language skills are still only at the level of class one?' In short, they thought that that school was entirely unsuitable for Kim and advised me to put him into the Jena-Plan school.

At the Jena-Plan school he went into class three again, because of his backwardness in reading and writing. I liked that class three teacher very much. I think that educators need to have some authority, they need to apply structure. But in between they must be able to bring to it lots of understanding and love. That was the case with her so things went like a bomb. Kim still had the odd angry outburst, but otherwise all was well. He was cheerful and full of high spirits. The therapy for his fears also helped somewhat.

A year later we had some bad luck, however. Kim found himself under a rather overwrought senior teacher who once pulled him along the corridor by his ears and other such pleasantries. Kim is a difficult child, you see, and there's no doubt he had done something that wasn't allowed: locking girls up in the toilet, I think. But that isn't something you should drag him right through the school for! I don't think you should allow yourself to do that sort of thing if you're a teacher. At any rate I then took Kim away from that school.

He went to a different school and he never wanted to do anything there. He also had difficulties with the teacher, but we managed to see things through and now he is in class three at the MAVO. A few years ago I went with him to a child psychiatric clinic because he was finding things so difficult. He was really bordering on the suicidal. They said: 'This boy should never have been allowed to go to the MAVO because his intelligence is such as would not shame the average professor'. But intelligence isn't everything, of course. I don't know to what extent his psychological problems have to do with dyslexia. The only thing I notice is that he clearly has difficulty with language skills. My children have got that from two sides, as both their father and I had similar problems. Even now my ex-husband still can't read. And Kim has just had another school report that shows an 8 for physics, a 7 for maths and a 7 for chemistry — and he doesn't do a stroke of work at them, you know; that MAVO is far too easy for him. But that report shows he got a 4 for German and a 4 for English. If I am to believe those psychologists, I've got super-intelligent children. But it doesn't get them anywhere. Somewhere there's something that stops it coming out, and what's even more important: something that makes them not very happy. Or at any rate particularly unstable and erratic. With Kees my impression is that he's unable to unlock his aptitude for the exact subjects and with Kim there are other things. For example, I feel that Kim is very musical and his violin lessons therefore went very well at the start. But after three years he still couldn't read any notes and then he didn't want to do it any more. And what are you to do then?

JEROEN

Of my third child, Jeroen, I can at least say that as far as I'm aware he is a happy child. As a baby he was a dear little thing, very quiet. It was only later that this changed. All he wanted to do was lie happily in the playpen until the big boys came home. Then he liked to sit up, but you had to help him as he was too lazy to do it for himself. He always sat watching what his big brothers were up to and he still looks up to them very much. His little sister Marieke doesn't do that at all; she stands up to them.

None of this takes away from the fact that at infants' school I talked to the infants' teacher because I wasn't totally confident about Jeroen. I said: 'All the same I'd like you to arrange to have him tested', as there were indications that he was going the same way as Kees and Kim. There were all kinds of series of things he didn't know — the days of the week, for instance, and the colours. I practised endlessly with him: 'The grass is green, Jeroen', but he simply couldn't grasp it. A minute later you could ask him: 'And what colour is the grass?' and then he'd stand there completely tongue-tied. The infants' school teacher said: 'Well, he must be colour-blind'. But he wasn't colour-blind in the slightest. He could see the difference perfectly well. It was simply that he couldn't remember the names. He didn't know the names of the children in his class either — a few he did but mostly he didn't. And in my opinion he's at least averagely intelligent, so that's crazy.

Then the infants' school teacher did all sorts of tests with him and she said: 'Actually, he is ready for school'. But you can understand why I was really concerned about it, certainly on the basis of my experiences with the first two. Fortunately in class one the teacher he got was a really pleasant man, some-what undemanding perhaps but an absolute dear. I said to him: 'Please pay attention to how things go with his spelling and distinguishing between the letters and so on'. Fortunately he was prepared to do that.

Then at the time of the first Christmas report he said to me: 'It's going splendidly. He does everything well. He's a little on the slow side, perhaps, but that's just how he is'. But in January or February he said: 'I've been keeping a close eye out again, and I think his ability to distinguish the letters of the alphabet isn't going well, not as I had expected. Perhaps it would be best if we brought the Schools Advisory Service (SAD)* in'. And that was done.

The SAD tested him and then said: 'There's nothing wrong, but perhaps he is simply imitating his eldest brother'. A brother who, mind you, is nearly ten years older! Well, I'm very sorry but that just won't wash. But in any case the SAD had the idea that the difficulties would be of a transitory nature. 'With a little extra attention he'll soon get over it'. They also said of Jeroen that he was terrifically intelligent. You can well imagine that I was gradually becoming somewhat chary.

Fortunately at the school there was a remedial teaching volunteer and she immediately took him on, and luckily when he reached class two that was able to continue. At first she said: 'Do you think we ought to do that, as things are going well now?' But I said: 'No, things aren't right yet. Something really ought to be happening'. I was panicking a little, because I was thinking: I don't want a second Kees in the house; I can't cope with that any more.

At the end of class two I again had a discussion, and the lady who was helping him wanted to keep on with him when he got to class three. The teacher he is with now has started to do class three dictations with him. On his report he got a 6– for them and she says: 'It really is a 6–'. So he's getting proper pass marks for them. Last year, you see, they'd also given him a 6– but that was a 'teaching figure'.

So things are going all right with Jeroen. With his school work, because for two years he has had two extra sessions a week to help to bring him up to standard, and in a psychological respect simply because things have worked out well for him. He has had understanding and yet at the same time stimulation. And those are precisely the two factors which my two elder boys had to get along without as far as school was concerned.

MARIEKE

What I had never thought was that my daughter would also have problems. She's always such a terrifically lively child. I thought she would just sail through everything. When she was eighteen months old she already knew 12 or 15 nursery rhymes by heart — the tunes, of course, without the words. She liked to sing and she still does, but the boys often say to her: 'Don't sit there moaning like that'. When she was small I would sing her a little song for her to go to sleep to. That was really very pleasant. And in fact she also started talking very early on. But now that she's in class two she too has reading and writing problems. Things are actually going better with reading than they did with the boys, but in general she is still at level one with her language skills when she ought to be at level four. A test showed that. But the test also showed that there were seven other children in her class who have the same problem: 7 out of 22. So the suspicion is that perhaps the fault lies in the teaching in that year. But then I said: 'But there are also children who are doing well'.

I simply don't know, but of course gradually I've become very alert. I can spot lots of differences compared to the boys. When Marieke was at infants' school, for instance, she always wanted to write down words. And now too she often sits reading. When the boys were at that stage they didn't care about that. They had no inclination to make any extra effort to do that. But she wants to be good.

That's why she also flies into one of her rages if she tries to write 'school' and doesn't manage to get the 's' right. That's something she has really badly, much worse than the boys. She often writes the 'p', the 'b', the 's' and the 'z' and similar letters the wrong way round. Then she grabs a new piece of paper only to do it wrong again. And then she sees that it won't work and becomes really enraged. So she's very ambitious. Sometimes this makes me think: 'She's just as badly affected as the boys but she tries harder to sort it out'. We can only hope that in her eagerness she isn't banging her head against a brick wall...

DYSLEXIA? YOU CAN CALL IT 'FULL MOON' IF YOU LIKE!

I myself was once tested by some centre or other and learnt that I was dyslexic. My parents were in education and I didn't have any trouble learning to read, but I couldn't get the spelling under my belt at all. In form two at secondary school I didn't go up to the next class because I had a 2, 3, 4 and 5 for my languages. But in the same report, for instance, there's also a 10 for maths!

There came a time, in form four, when I stopped going to school. I put it all to one side and in addition there were other big problems. But later when I got older I took a professional training course. I became a nurse. The crazy thing is that I can now write letters that are completely free of mistakes! So perhaps I've grown out of it. Mind you, I do have difficulty if I'm checking dictations that the children have done. But if I write it out myself I know whether it is correct. Perhaps more attention used to be paid to spelling at primary school when I was a child. It was simply rammed in.

When Kees was in form one I therefore told the Child and Family Guidance Clinic that in my opinion he had the same thing — dyslexia. But they don't like it at all when you come up with it. And later when he was in form five they said: 'We don't want to stick that label on him'. Then I said: 'I couldn't care less whether you call it "peanut butter" or "full moon" as long as you do something about it'. But in fact they always failed to do anything. They meant well but they knew very little about it. I therefore always felt I was very much on my own.

Unfortunately I couldn't afford to go to all kinds of expensive testing agencies to get it investigated properly. With Kees

alone I was already spending money on extra lessons, homework courses and so on. We were living below the social security minimum and for two years I spent all the spare cash I had
on extra lessons. For years we couldn't even afford any clothes.

Of course, I've always done exercises with my children
myself: with Kees, for example, when his reading wasn't going
smoothly. I know now that you must never read above a child's
level, but I didn't know it then. All I could think of then was:
practice, practice, practice. We did it like this: I would read a
paragraph out and then he was allowed to do a little piece. As
he did so I always larded on the praise.

But the school told me that the reason he wasn't reading
well was that I was pushing him too hard. The worst thing you
could do as a mother was work with your children. In retrospect
I have to say that it always went enjoyably. We had the best of
relationships as we worked. The things that went between us
cannot have been bad for the child. They always give this standard advice! However, that then made me so unsure of myself
that I immediately stopped, and after that I never read with him
again.

Do you know what is also so wretched? When they are
doing what they enjoy, children like mine who are reasonably
intelligent quickly find themselves so far above the level of
what they can read that it is terribly difficult to get them to read
at all. My children didn't even want to tackle those large-print
books. At that time I used to go to the library every week with
Kees. I didn't force anything, but I would say: 'Gosh, that looks
nice. Why don't you just try it?' But mostly he didn't read a
single page of it.

Do you know when he started reading? When we had got
hold of *The Little Captain* by Paul Biegel. He thought that was
marvellous. He read all three parts off his own bat and now
Jeroen is getting lots of pleasure out of reading them. That's
just the sort of boy he is.

Last year, in a relatively short period — at any rate for him
— he read the Tolkien books, *Lord of the Rings*. They're really
thick and difficult books. But he read them, although apart from
those he never reads anything else. Of course, I bought the

books then, as once he's got through a book he likes to read it five times. I think that is because he doesn't read everything first time through. That's how it was when he was smaller too, when I used to read with him.

Often it would go like this: he would spell a word out and then make something of it. And if he read the sentence over again he would come up with a word that wasn't there at all but which fitted the sense. Sometimes it would even be a synonym. For example it might say 'ship' and he would make it into 'boat'. That's how he reads. In a story that is often not so bad. At a certain moment he is able to grasp the essence of the narrative. Not all the details, of course. But to do foreign languages like that, or to know whether you're supposed to calculate the circumference or the surface area, that's quite a different matter. And it's in those areas that everything therefore gets confused for Kees.

In form one of the secondary technical school where Kees is now, the children were all tested for their language skills. I recently had a note saying the test had shown that he is having great difficulty in that area. Each week the school is going to give him extra teaching, but, as they wrote in the note, 'that is no guarantee that all will turn out well'. It therefore looks as though the school is going to take steps of its own accord. That is something which has never happened before with any of my four children.

I have always had to find everything out for myself. Often I've been pushed from pillar to post. What I always found particularly frustrating was the uncertainty about whether you're doing the right thing. For a while this created all sorts of difficulties for me. But all I know is that every time I had to take a decision I had made all the enquiries possible and obtained all the possible information. I discussed each step with all sorts of people who I thought had a point of view to contribute.

Undoubtedly wrong decisions have been made and from time to time I've felt waves of guilt come over me about them. But I've done everything with the best of intentions. In those confusing situations I often didn't know the right direction to take. I still don't, actually. Because where am I to go now, with my depressive Kees? He is in the middle of puberty and has great emotional problems. He really ought to have specialist help but at the moment he doesn't want anything else at all. I am really anxious, because he gives such a dozy, sleepy impression. There is a block somewhere, but what should I do: should I now tackle the language skills or ought we first to work on his closeness, his reticence?

Perhaps I ought simply to go along to that intermediate technical school, but do you know what the problem is? I have four children and there is something the matter with all of them. Also I have a busy job which takes a lot of my energy. And then sometimes I'm sitting at home and the little ones have to go to bed and I think to myself: Again that teacher hasn't rung me up. Shall I ring him at home? What was his name again? And before you know where you are it's ten o'clock. I simply don't succeed all the time. It becomes too much for me, gradually I find I can no longer put myself out to do it.

Commentary by Specialists

PSYCHOLOGICAL AND EMOTIONAL FACTORS SOMETIMES OVERSHADOW THE DYSLEXIC PICTURE

It is undeniable that dyslexia, which ought in fact to be an isolated problem, sometimes overflows into other areas, overshadowing a child's whole life. The frequency and extent to which this happens is not known exactly, because the great majority of these problems are not classified as dyslexia. In the long term the psychological and emotional aspects get the upper hand and the real cause can no longer be traced. Where the difficulties can be classified as 'dyslexia' it is generally possible to keep track of them. It sometimes seems as if this simple designation confines the problem to where it ought to be: reading and writing.

Yet one knows stories of people who are finally able to explain the psychological and emotional problems which they used to have to struggle with by the fact that they were dyslexic. Often the pieces in the puzzle did not fall into place until they themselves had children, who were better taken care of because the nature of their problems was recognised earlier. There is every reason to suppose that even nowadays a lot of hidden psychological suffering can be laid at the door of dyslexia.

This is not surprising given the nature of this handicap. In the previous chapter we explained that the specific gifts of dyslexic people are often at odds with what society — or at any rate the school — expects from them. As a dyslexic child, of course, you may find yourself at a school where you have fallen on your feet; the problem is recognised or at any rate there is an understanding of it, however abstract. There is no attempt to pigeon-hole you; you are valued for what you are, with your strengths and weaknesses. This form of acceptance also subsequently helps you to accept the problems which you will inevitably have to face.

But what if your environment is not so understanding? One's parents to start with, of course, although in most cases we can assume they will continue to support their child. But what if at school you encounter a rigid teacher of the old style who wants to pump into you what just won't go? You can hear about people like that in all the stories that dyslexic people tell, and they can make you or break you. We all depend during our lives on the people we happen to come across, but dyslexic children are defined by them to a greater extent.

Thus for example a phenomenon can occur which can be given the rather fashionable name of 'fear of failure'. A child who is repeatedly confronted by failures will in the long term think he or she is absolutely incapable of anything, and so the other school subjects start to suffer from the handicap. A dyslexic child is regarded as stupid and consequently also starts to consider themselves as stupid. Now if a child like this really was stupid, perhaps there would not be anything so bad in this. But under the surface the realisation is always smouldering that one can do more, that one is not realising one's potential. The intelligence that is there is just not being expressed, and it may then look for another outlet. One cannot predict whether that will be in the form of difficult behaviour or internal psychological or emotional conflicts. That depends on the child's own personality. One might be a fighter who will not give in and will then start to behave unacceptably. And another — the escaper — suppresses it all and, for example, transforms it into irrational fears or infantile behaviour. Whatever the case, the eventual symptoms are often miles away from where it all started: the dyslexia. Even professional helpers will not always be able to pierce this mask. And in this way a period of extremely unpleasant struggle is initiated in which the dyslexia has completely disappeared into the background. It no longer plays any role at all.

In these cases too, however, the 'chance people' one meets can offer a solution. Often you see a child pick up under an understanding teacher, only perhaps to slip back into previous behaviour in the next class under a less suitable figure. With problems of this type it is therefore less important to trace the cause in the first instance. What comes first is offering 'first aid' in the form of recognition, respect, confidence and understanding. Once the explosive situation has then stabilised somewhat, one can go in search of the background.

QUESTIONS

Do all dyslexic children have to struggle with emotional problems?

Dyslexia is seldom wholly unaccompanied by emotional problems. After all, children themselves, just like their parents, have certain expectations about their achievements at school. These expectations will probably partly be based on how they get on with their contemporaries — the feeling of being able to keep abreast of them, and not being different. If this feeling of being normal is slowly frustrated in the course of time because certain things are not going as they should or are going with great difficulty, problems will arise. The question: 'Why can't I do this? I'm perfectly intelligent in other ways' will not present itself consciously in the case of many primary school children, but subconsciously it nevertheless causes tensions. And if a child is placed in a different school or receives special help, the feeling that they are 'different' is reinforced. In the family too the additional attention which the child with learning difficulties receives can come to form a problem.

The emotional problems which arise out of the perceived incapacity and the child's exceptional position can vary, however, from slight to very serious. If dyslexic children are well catered for at home and at school, the various aspects can be kept within reasonable bounds. And even if all does not go so smoothly at school, a child will often derive enormous security from the support given at home.

In addition how children respond to their difficulties depends to an appreciable extent on their personality structure. Some children refuse to be bested by anything or anybody and others again are more sensitive to frustrations. How cautiously one ought to cater for a child's problems will depend on the type of child.

CHAPTER 8

Between the Devil and the Deep Blue Sea

Does our Educational System Attach more Importance to Children's Deficiencies than to their Positive Qualities?

In this chapter parents of dyslexic children relate the problems they face when trying to find suitable secondary schools for their children. Sometimes the obstacles are those they have already run up against in relation to primary schools. Put briefly, what it comes down to is that dyslexic children do not seem to fit into most educational regimes. Either too much is asked of them, so that they become afraid of failure and become under-achievers on all fronts, or else too little is asked of them, and then they just fall asleep intellectually.

That is the drama of children who are unilaterally gifted: they do not fit in at schools which elevate the average as the norm. Joris's and Wendela's parents therefore sought a way out by looking for schools for their children which had individual approaches. There, the argument goes, at least all the facets of their children's abilities will be given their due, both the weak sides and the strong ones.

It took some searching, however, before these parents determined on their choice, as schools of that kind are by no means thick on the ground and in addition they are often some way below the level which parents and child consider desirable. This is the concession which has to be made to the individual approach.

The question therefore is: is it not possible to make appropriate choices for dyslexic children at all levels of their intellectual functioning? Or is it their fate always to be assessed on the weakest link in the chain of their scholastic attainments? Are there, in fact, schools which have an eye for their positive qualities?

The Parents of Joris (Aged 13) tell their Story

WEAK AND STRONG SIDES

When Joris was four we moved to South America. There he attended the local infants' school. There was a time when, of course, he spoke all the languages mixed up together, but that signified little.

When we returned he was nearly six, and here in Holland they said: 'He is not ready for school'. We asked: What is it he can't do? Well, it turned out he couldn't count up to ten and he didn't know the colours. Also, he couldn't button up his jacket on his own. That figured, because he hadn't worn a jacket for months. And at private schools in South America of the kind he had attended there are lots of girl helpers running around doing everything for the children. If a child drops a shoe she'll pick it up. Certainly they never put on their jackets themselves.

He could do other things, though. We had travelled and flown a lot and he had become quite adept at that sort of thing — finding his way around airports and so on. I think if we had put him down at any airport and said to him: 'Joris, here's a ticket to Tokyo, and from there you've to go to New York', he would have got there. That's something he *could* do. So we said to the school: 'You must be more specific', as all they were giving us were rather vague criticisms. Now they were very bad at doing that. They said: 'It would be best for Joris if he simply did a year at infants' school over again'. But we said: 'Then you must come up with a plan, because just playing with wooden blocks for another year won't hold his interest'.

The fact is we could also see that there were a number of things that were not quite as they ought to be. But the infants' school merely said: 'Well, the counting and the colours you must do yourselves. That's not part of our role'. And then we thought: 'If we have to do it ourselves anyway, he might as well go to primary school'. It turned out that the burden fell on our own shoulders. We went off to the primary school and said: 'Will you take a child who has got such-and-such problems?' Well, they would give it a try. But in fact we could see straight away that it wouldn't work. But what the problem was we didn't actually know.

The primary school said: 'It'll turn out all right'. And in the second year: 'He's a tremendously nice boy. His reading and writing are hopeless but he's such a pleasant child. It'll all be OK!' Then the third year. Halfway through it we asked: 'Are things turning out all right yet?' 'Nice boy, isn't he?' was the answer. 'But are things turning out all right?' we asked. 'Oh yes!' 'No', we said, 'we don't now think it *is* going to put itself right of its own accord'. Meanwhile we had started to talk about it rather more to an acquaintance of ours who was a teacher. She was also doing a training course as a remedial teacher and one for learning and educational problems. So she knew quite a lot about it. We asked her: 'Do you think he'll make up the ground?' 'No, of course not, that's nonsense'. Well, that was the feeling we had had too.

And at the end of the third year we said to the school: 'There's got to be some intervention now'. In the fourth year the Schools Advisory Service (SBD) came into the picture. They said: 'We think this is a case of dyslexia'. That was something that had meanwhile already occurred to us. Because Joris could analyse the words into letters but he could never manage the next stage and make a proper word out of them. If you read with him he fantasised. He evidently thought: that must be what it's about. Sometimes he would guess right but often he missed the target by a mile.

The education advisory service discovered that there were other children in Joris's class who were dyslexic. So they drew up a plan for him and the others. On Friday afternoon the class one teacher did extra work with Joris and the other children. Reading exercises and suchlike. At home we also did a great deal on it. We did every possible word game. We made up crossword puzzles ourselves, for instance. Even in the holidays we always took special games with us.

You could tell that it was helping. The dictations were going better. There were no longer always 25 mistakes; the number was reduced to 20. And so he went up into class five. There once again things didn't go smoothly, so once more we set the alarm bells ringing. We said: 'Teachers, don't behave as if there's nothing wrong. There is'. Again we talked to the education advisory service and they said: 'Hmm, actually he needs to be tested in a better way. We don't have the facilities to do that. There is no money for it. That can only be done in the first three years. So you'll need to have that done privately'. We then said to each other: 'It can be done here at home', but all the same you experience it as a nasty trick, since we were the ones who'd first sounded the alarm! All the time they had dragged the matter out and put it off.

This school always collaborates with a bureau which advises on school and career choices, but we didn't have a very high opinion of it at all. Our eldest daughter had also been tested there, you see, and it was definitely not a very pleasant place. So we engaged a different one. We put two very specific questions to them. Firstly: 'Does Joris suffer from dyslexia and if so what can we do about it?' And secondly: 'How do we get through his remaining years at primary school?'

The consultants went into those questions very thoroughly. We received a diagnostic report and a recommendation. They said: 'It's a form of dyslexia'. That was very clear. By then it was already January/February, so he had another year and a half to go at primary school. The recommendation was that when we saw the opportunity — in consultation with the education advisory service and the school — Joris should be kept back a year. 'Either in class five or in class six', they said. At that time we would need to implement a special programme for him. But they also said: 'If you think it is bothering him, or if he can't manage in the group or in the system, then it isn't absolutely essential for him to be kept back a year'.

Finally in consultation with the school we decided not to keep Joris back. You see, his intelligence is quite high and the education advisory service and the school said: 'It'll become boring for him'. We used the remaining year and a half well, to complete the programme. Also at that time he started reading like a maniac. It started with *Willie Wonka and the Chocolate Factory*. That book really got him going. And after that he went on to read *Chameleons* (a series of Dutch children's books).

Apart from those special books, he's also reading ordinary books now. But he reads in fits and starts. He can read three new books on the trot and then for a while he gets no further than his strip cartoons and his *Chameleons*. He can re-read those endlessly.

YOU HAVE TO DRAW OUT WHAT'S IN THERE

In class five it turned out that Joris had an IQ of about 120. That's some way above average. So immediately and very critically we posed the question: 'Do you think he'll find most of the subjects challenging, at the Lower Horticulture School* for example?' 'No', the man at the testing bureau said with great frankness, 'he would probably be bored to tears there'. But nor did he have any answer to the question of what in fact we ought to do with Joris as far as his secondary education was concerned.

So there we were. Meanwhile the exercises got off to a good start. He worked with a number of cards. The biggest problem for him was the consonants — sit, sitting and so on. It's something he still has difficulty with. He never knows whether 'sits' ought to have two t's or not.

Just yesterday we were sitting playing Scrabble. He can do that as well as anyone else, because we often play it. He was able to put down the word 'income', but he said: 'It has two m's, doesn't it? If it has I can't put it down'. He can't work out for himself that it only has one 'm'. You can let him think about it for an hour and a quarter but he still won't get there.

At any rate he practised the vowels and consonants quite a lot at school, besides doing his ordinary schoolwork. All the same, of course, his reading and writing still didn't progress all that well. And then you have to keep saying to the teachers: 'Do you think it's realistic to mark Joris's dictations like everybody else's?' You wouldn't have somebody with a physical handicap doing the Four Day Walking Event. So we think that with a dyslexic child you ought to apply different standards.

After some urging on our part they then went over to giving him a 'teaching mark'. At that school you could be assessed not only on your progress but also on your effort and we'd already noticed a few times on reports that these figures went up in the same way. There was a linear connection between them. Well, there's something odd about that, we thought. After all, some children make great strides with little effort. And others, like Joris with his dictations, make great efforts but only progress slowly. They took rather more account of that during his last year at the school.

Then came the crucial moment: the achievement test at the end of primary school. We deliberately didn't inform the testing organisation about it in detail. We thought: let them simply look at it. But when it was time to go and discuss it with them, the head of the school said to the assessment bureau: 'These are parents who are well aware of the problems. The question they will ask is: what education is there that is suitable for this child? And don't come up with vocational education, as they won't put up with that. Consider thoroughly what options there are for Joris, as that's something they will definitely ask'.

We arrived there and the man said: 'Mm, a problem with reading and writing, eh? Level of class three and no higher, eh?' 'Look', we said, 'we know that. But what education can the local authority now actually offer?' 'Now that I really wouldn't know'. Then we said, 'We understand. It's something we'll have to research ourselves'. People like that are terribly irritating. And they make out they're a school and vocational assessment organisation!

So they simply didn't know what to do for that sort of child. They'd simply never considered it! Above-average intelligence and dyslexic — do you mean to say that combination occurs quite often? One child in ten seems to have this sort of problem and on average dyslexic children are no less intelligent than others.

r*e

Yet the bulk of them are evidently just packed off to the lower vocational school (LBO). Or at any rate some course where their strengths don't get an opportunity to shine.

So the level of education is actually matched to a child's lowest-scoring capacities. Our educational system is incapable of providing children with this defect with an intellectual challenge. Nor do most parents, of course, know where they ought to be looking. Some suffer from the delusion that their children are simply none too clever, as a child's other skills are often just snowed under. Then you have to be a real termagant if you want to track down the real cause of your child's reading and writing problems. And even that hardly gets you any further on, because in fact nobody knows what the answer is for this kind of child. It really is crazy — after so many years of assessment it is as if you're the first parent to come up with this kind of thing!

At any rate it was clear that the problem was being foisted off onto us, so we got hold of a local authority guide listing all the schools each with a description. We leafed through it endlessly, with a street map of the town next to it, as of course you can't have children travelling too far.

We started out with the proposition that you need to draw out what is in the child. There are limits to what is possible, but Joris is not to go to the lower vocational school just because he happens to be dyslexic. He really is absolutely unsuited to it. You see, he isn't really all that skilful with his hands. But he does have understanding. So he can sit for ages examining how he can make pumps and things of that kind using his technical Lego. But at the lower vocational school he will be absolutely bored stiff as far as a subject like maths is concerned!

Eventually we stumbled on the leaflet from the Montessori school. There it said in as many words: we can help children with dyslexia. So off we went to the open day at the Montessori school. 'Yes, indeed', they said, 'we do have those facilities here. We are structured for it'. They did add in all frankness: 'Of course, one teacher will have more of a feeling for it than another. And there are also some who are not so keen on it'.

We registered Joris officially in January. Not long after that we were called for a discussion with the guidance counsellor for the bridging year. He also said: 'Yes, we can help children with dyslexia'. They only had HAVO and VWO*; there was no MAVO department but they were going to arrange a merger with a Montessori MAVO. And they said: 'In view of his report he's probably a MAVO pupil. If he wasn't dyslexic then of course things would have been different'.

All the same in that discussion it was more or less promised that Joris would be allowed to try the HAVO. Because of the merger, transferring was always still possible. That was at the end of January. February, March, April — we heard nothing more. And we said to ourselves: 'It'll all be going through, of course'. But at the end of April all of a sudden there was a letter: 'Dear Parents, we are extremely sorry but in view of his capabilities we believe that Joris is not suited to the HAVO. We are unable to admit him'.

That was at the end of April! By then every other child was already enrolled at a school. Most schools had even closed their enrolment period. And Joris had already been telling everyone: 'I'm going to the Montessori school — it's going to be really great'. You can well imagine that we were nearer to crying than laughing.

Nevertheless we had to do something. By now we knew the local authority's guide by heart and it was clear to us that there was absolutely no point now in trying an ordinary HAVO. Meanwhile our eldest daughter was also having difficulties in that direction — probably as a result of puberty — and then you quickly realise that that extra little bit of help is lacking.

Then we decided to send him to an IVO-MAVO. Admittedly there they said: 'We're not structured for it', but we said: 'It isn't necessary for you to be. So long as you have an understanding of the problem'. And they do! When Joris had been at the school for a while, the school went to the local authority and said: 'It's our impression that we have other children like this'. They got money to enable teachers to go to the dyslexia conference. In addition they used that little nest-egg to appoint a psychologist who tested all the children in forms one and two who were facing this kind of problem. The three hours which they still have left they will be using to instruct the foreign language teachers on the question: how do you teach dyslexic children?

The Father of Wendela (Aged 13) tells his Story

WE'RE DOING OUR BEST AS FAR AS THE DICTATIONS ARE CONCERNED!

When we realised at the end of the fourth year that Wendela was dyslexic I really got the feeling I was looking through a keyhole at my own past. It made lots of things fall into place as in a jigsaw puzzle. Of course it would be wrong to attribute everything to a single factor, but in retrospect I have the idea that my life has been very strongly determined by it.

Only now is my peculiar, lop-sided education becoming clear. Not being able to keep up in languages at the MULO*, and then building up for your career later via lower technical school and evening classes and that sort of thing. In fact, you see, the intelligence is there, but the specific avenue of classical education runs at cross-purposes to it.

For a month it really rattled me when I realised that I myself was also dyslexic. All sorts of youthful memories came floating to the surface. Tears and events which came back to me like a series of photographs. But at the time I kept very quiet and calm. As a child I made few friends. A single one, perhaps. And I see Wendela following the same strategy: above all trying not to be conspicuous, because if you are conspicuous you run risks. Floating along with the stream is the strategy.

So there must be other children at primary schools who try to struggle along through their school life like little grey mice. I think there are at least three children at Wendela's primary school who are in the same situation. But then you often see how reticent parents are in conceding to themselves that they have a problem. Because you need to be quite fanatical to get to the bottom of it!

In Wendela's case, of course, it was as clear as daylight that something was wrong. You could see from every angle that she was a very intelligent child who was blocked because her means of expression were so one-sided. And that was assessed. The other side is very under-illuminated. Concentration on achievement is so central in most school systems! There is still absolutely no inkling of the possibility of a more stimulating approach.

So you as parents have to counter it very regularly. On the one hand you have to act very diplomatically so as not to offend the school, and on the other you have to score so as to make the situation such that your child is in a slightly more favourable starting position. Sometimes we were hesitantly given some cooperation. They would say to us: 'We're glad not all the parents are like you, because if they were we really wouldn't be able to cope'.

You see, the situation is that dyslexia also has implications other than those thrown up by dictations. As far as dictations were concerned the teacher had a good understanding of the problem. He was prepared to put wavy lines under the right words instead of under the wrong ones. And he never gave Wendela marks for dictations. But when you try to maintain that it also has effects on topography, the learning of definitions, or recorder lessons, well... then what you get is something along the lines of: 'Now we're doing our best as far as the dictations are concerned!' It is clear that regular education in general is not oriented towards people's characteristics. Certainly not towards those which the future demands. In general people's thinking is very linear: the children start here and you deliver them there. This is the starting level and that's what we require by the end. But the knowledge which needs to be acquired nowadays is no longer so linear. It is much more important to teach children to understand the content. This applies to all children, of course, but dyslexic children particularly are the victims of this approach. I found it very typical, for instance, that in class six Wendela was tested for pre-university education (VWO) but on the basis of the figures she ought to have gone for lower vocational education (LBO)! And for her that's no challenge at all. I myself absolutely terrorised the class for two years at the lower technical school (LTS).

So there came a time with Wendela when we were at a terrible break point, in class six of primary school. Things continued to go badly and even individual remedial teaching wasn't helping. As far as the ordinary secondary education was concerned she had come to a complete and utter stop. Yet at the LBO school her strong sides would still not be able to express themselves.

Then in a crazy panic we rang up all the Remedial Schools in the area. But one of them said: 'It will not be of any benefit to get this child into a Remedial School, because we cannot cope with her either. She's too far above our level. We have only three to five per cent of children who go on to the MAVO. And then the gulf between your child and the others will be too great'.

So that Remedial School was conceding that there were also children who fall outside its area of expertise. They cannot cater for all learning difficulties. Originally I thought the Remedial School was intended for normal intelligent children. But the level has clearly fallen. The social problems have come to occupy a more central place. There are also so many variants of children and so many gradations...

What you must therefore look for, if your child belongs to one of those variants, is a school where the children are given an individual approach. At least you can then be sure that your child's specific qualities will be given their due and that at any rate the child won't just be lumped together with the rest. Finally, therefore, we sent our Wendela to a school which is linked with an educational institute. What they have is a form of special education for children who otherwise threaten to fall between the devil and the deep blue sea. You must really regard it as a sort of bridge to regular education. At the school where Wendela now is they are trying to equip her sufficiently in one or two years, both emotionally and intellectually, to be able to hold her own in normal secondary education.

UNDERSTANDING AND STIMULATION

The difference between Wendela at primary school and Wendela now is best illustrated by the fact that within two days she was one of the editors of the school newspaper. In the very first week she was busy at my desk writing an article. Now: Wendela and writing! That would have been completely out of order previously.

Although she's always made attempts, she never received any praise for it. So her efforts didn't make it to the school newspaper. Recently she took the new school newspaper to her old head teacher — my impression is that it was really to get even with her. She's written four articles in it and she was never allowed to write for the old school newspaper.

Formerly the system was that each child was allowed to make a contribution to it once a year. Hers was then reduced to a very short piece, whilst others were given extensive space. And Wendela is a very sensitive child who feels every nuance of that kind of treatment. The way she put that was: 'I make too many mistakes so my pieces aren't allowed to go in'.

That is so different from her present school system! One continually points out your mistakes and the other tries to stimulate you as much as possible. You may be lucky, of course, and at primary school be one of those pupils who are high achievers on all fronts. Those children will experience few obstacles under that system; it's really been thought up for them. But a dyslexic child...

Wendela always used to come home from primary school exhausted, miserable and peevish. And that's just not part of the picture now, though it is an hour's journey each way by bus. In the three months that she has now been at the school she has really taken an enormous step forward in her development. It is just as if she is firmly back on her feet again. It's really staggering!

Partly, of course, you can say it's just the phase of life that she's at. But in fact it is too unexpected for that, and too rapid. After three weeks the germ of it was already there. One knows theoretically that it can work like that, but to see that in your own child was very moving. The nice thing about her school is that they do not make it really easy for her. They can be pretty strict. There has to be achievement. They say: 'You must do your homework. How many mistakes there are in it is not the point, but we must have evidence that you're doing your best'. And if she doesn't work she gets a good telling off.

Dyslexia and other learning disturbances are, of course, difficult topics to get to grips with from a teaching point of view. On the one hand you must be able to understand that a child simply cannot meet certain requirements, or can only meet them with great difficulty. But on the other hand this kind of child must also be stimulated. Demands must be made on her. At this school I think it is very clear that they have found that balance.

They rely partly on the discipline of learning. After all, it is a very important requirement if one is to get back into regular education. They keep the problem very close to the child herself. They make it clear to her that she is responsible for her own life, that she really can somehow fight her way through it. I think that is very good. It has also produced results in Wendela's case.

The capacity to persevere is trained in all kinds of ways, including physical ones. They have the children run quite a distance, for example. And in her second week at that school there was a survival camp. They had to cross a stream using ropes. And there was a day's canoeing. Activities of that kind.

Partly, of course, the lessons are oriented towards children who will go on to vocational education, but thirty per cent of pupils from this school nevertheless go to some form or other of secondary general education. There is a good chance that Wendela will also be among those. And from experience I know that if you're dyslexic there's only one way you make progress: simply by wading in and carving out your own path. That's exactly what Wendela is now learning at this school.

It therefore doesn't matter very much to me about the precise approach they adopt. There seem to be various currents, but at that school they are fairly interconnected. The most important thing for me is: so long as the basis is laid in the form

of an ability to rescue you from yourself — regaining confidence — as Wendela's self-confidence had been seriously shak-
en by the end of primary school.

For instance, what hurt me greatly is that the negative stories about the primary school only came out when she had just
got to this school. I found it awful to hear things like: 'I didn't
like this and I didn't like that'. But later I thought: perhaps she
also suppressed a number of things at primary school. They
simply caused her too much pain. During that time she simply
switched off her feelings.

Wendela (Aged 13) tells her Story

THE NEW SCHOOL

At ten past seven each morning I am collected by the bus
and at quarter past four in the afternoon I'm back home again.
I'm the only girl on the bus and most of the children are older,
but I enjoy myself. I sleep a bit or I try to learn sign language.
You see, there are a lot of deaf children there.

We have small classes at the new school, so we are all
given a great deal of attention. I'm in a class of seven children.
There is a teacher who teaches reading, writing and arithmetic.
He always says: 'In arithmetic we don't learn that one and one
makes two but we teach you the mnemonics'. He teaches you
how you can remember it, or how you can find it out for yourself. His name is Hans. We're allowed to call all the teachers by
their first names, only the co-ordinator do we call by his sur-
name. If we say 'Charles' to him he thinks we're being cheeky.

The subjects we are taught are biology, gym, arithmetic
— I don't know any maths but once you have finished with
arithmetic you can do maths. Very many children have forgotten some of the material from the primary school, so we're getting that first at the moment, but I think that counting will go
very smoothly for me. I don't really yet know, as we've only
just started on it. At Christmas we get our first reports... Then
we also have sentence analysis, reading, writing, dictations,

drawing, geography, physics, handicrafts, music and cookery. Actually, cookery is called 'domestic science'. And geography and history we get at the same time. They are together in one book. And then there is also speech therapy, but I have that on my own.

Speech therapy is to help you to pronounce things properly. She's always hammering away at the f's and the v's. I don't know exactly because I can't hear it. But that's what she keeps saying. And also where the 'h' and the 'p' are in your mouth. But how does that help you? What difference does it make if you know where the 'h' is formed? I know perfectly well how to pronounce them! And also she isn't really a nice lady...

I also have physiotherapy, but that will probably stop after Christmas. Often we use two balls, throwing and catching at the same time. Standing on a block and throwing them down. Or sitting in a strange position. Then another child has to imitate it. And if he does it wrong you have to give him instructions. You mustn't touch him but you have to tell him exactly. So you yourself have to remember exactly how you were sitting. Then I have to say something like: 'No, your right arm needs to be lower' and things like that. And left and right I do find difficult. I have a very odd way of remembering that. I can wink much better with my right eye than with my left. So if I now momentarily forget, that's what I try to do. And then I think: that belongs with that shoulder so that is that arm.

They're not so keen on marks at this school. But there are a few children in my class who always like to have a mark. So that is what they get. But you don't get a report with marks on it. The report simply says how far you are on with each subject. We did have a few marks for domestic science, though. For how you clean up after cooking, and for cleaning cupboards and pans. I've already twice had a 10 for that!!! And a 9.5 for physics! Next time we're going to make something in domestic science and then the teacher's going to try it. We have to beat everything by hand and not use an electric mixer or anything like that. If children cannot beat very well there's something wrong with their motor skills, I believe. In any case they then pass that on to the physiotherapy lady and the child has to do some exercises. The teachers talk about us a lot to each other. Once a month there is consultation between all the teachers on every child.

The marvellous thing is this, I think: at the new school they don't count in the language mistakes with the other subjects. They only say: it does need to be fairly legible. My present geography teacher doesn't like doing topography, fortunately, because at that other school I could never remember all those difficult words. And now I sometimes write things down completely wrongly. But she says: 'As long as I understand what you mean'. With dictations we really do get a lot more time to read them over. At primary school we were also allowed to read them over, but by the time you had to hand them in I'd only reached the third line. Here you simply get enough time until you've finished.

I'm now in an A0 group. That is to do extra work on what you're behind in. And a B0 group is to work further on that. And then you have A1, there some new subjects are added, and B1 are the same subjects but just that bit more difficult. If you are through the O^e group, you choose LBO or MAVO. A1 is LBO and B1 are the first few subjects of MAVO.

Perhaps I'll stay here just for two years and then go on to the ordinary HAVO. Or if I still can't go to the HAVO, two years at the MAVO first. Later I want to go to stage school. At the other school we had plays. I don't find it all that difficult to learn a story by heart. Words I do find hard. But at primary school they always thought: 'She's unable to learn very well, so we won't give her a leading part'. I thought that was a great pity, because I do at least want to be an actress and that's why I DO WANT TO GO TO THE HAVO!

Commentary by Specialists

THE REALITY OF SECONDARY EDUCATION

The transition from primary school to secondary education is a big step for any child, but for children with learning difficulties it sometimes seems an unbridgeable gulf. Admittedly that cannot be blamed only on the children or on the learning problems. The structure and organisation at secondary schools are after all such that only the strongest children can hold their own.

From the relative protection of the primary school environment twelve- and thirteen-year-old children are suddenly confronted by a multiplicity of different subjects and teachers, by homework which the teachers give independently of each other, so that one subject sometimes suffers because of another, by a murderously fast pace compared to primary school, by tests which can sometimes signify enormous emotional pressure, by foreign languages which are often taught in very different ways and each of which therefore requires its own approach. And in addition the child is in the early phases of puberty.

Once you take stock of this list it is surprising that a child is to any extent able to negotiate this transition without experiencing learning problems. But a child who enters secondary education on a precarious basis will at most schools fall mercilessly through the net. Whereas at primary school the language problem can be reduced to a relatively small part of the total function of schooling, at secondary school it suddenly expands to encompass all the subjects. In all areas one has to read and write. The time pressure is immense and most dyslexic children will discover right from the start that they are never able to finish the task in time. As a result, in all probability they will start to work more sloppily, skipping over things, not reading the text fully or completely disregarding it. Moreover, whilst the technical aspects of reading and writing often still demand considerable attention, often the child cannot process the content of the material offered. Connections in the text often pass them by. They cannot apply the material that is being taught. Their memories become overloaded and allow things to be forgotten. In addition they are often confronted by problems of confrontation and motivation.

This may be a somewhat depressing picture of secondary education, but for a great many dyslexic children it is the hard reality. How things could be is another matter. We will return in a subsequent chapter to what teachers with a little goodwill can do about the often insuperable problems of dyslexic children in secondary education.

Here the question arises whether at secondary school dyslexic children do in fact have prospects that match their actual capacities. The answer is a resounding yes, always providing...

Bearing in mind the major obstacles, it does make sense to give these children more time, without thereby giving them the idea that they are failures. In this way one can decide to let them climb up via the longer route of LEAO*–MAVO–HAVO so that they end up at the right point all the same.

Another option is for these pupils to be intensively coached by a professional specialising in dyslexia. He or she can help the pupil to adopt an appropriate attitude, encourage the right learning behaviour and attempt to channel the problem into those areas that are the ones actually involved: reading and spelling (now including the reading and spelling of foreign languages). Remedial help is only sensible, however, if the pupils themselves also see its usefulness and are motivated to cooperate, so it is best to start as early as possible and not wait until the pupil has become completely bogged down.

QUESTIONS

Is it known whether an intellect which is potentially there can fall asleep if it is not stimulated enough?

Research in relation to animals and humans has shown that the environment exerts a clear influence on the structure and function of the brain. This influence can be both stimulating and inhibiting or even destructive in nature.

Very young children especially are receptive to environmental influences of all kinds. Their brains are structurally and functionally not yet fully grown and can still adapt to an appreciable extent to the demands made on them. People used to talk of certain 'critical periods' in which the adaptation concerned necessarily took place if a certain aspect of development was to proceed. Nowadays this is viewed rather less rigidly, but it remains a fact that if the brain is deprived of the necessary stimuli — for example visual stimuli, by blindfolding a baby for a long period — the function concerned — in this case seeing — cannot develop optimally.

Whereas this applies to physical stimuli, it can be presumed that the teaching and mental environment also play important roles with regard to the development of the brain. Although much less is known about the precise effects of these complex influences than about those of simple stimuli, nevertheless their importance is generally recognised. It can therefore be considered not improbable that in the case of a dyslexic child who is insufficiently stimulated in the areas in which he or she *is* good a certain regression of function will take place. On the other hand exercising both strengths and weaknesses can be expected to produce favourable results in this regard.

Apart from the question of whether an intellect will remain functionally or even structurally underdeveloped or will even regress if not given enough teaching stimuli, in a completely different area the child's motivation for the areas of knowledge concerned also plays a role in the intellect's apparently falling asleep. In the case of highly gifted children, for instance, it is well known that they often perform only moderately because the teaching material does not challenge them sufficiently. Dyslexic children who have to perform below their top level in their strong areas will finish up in a comparable situation. It is therefore quite possible that part of the unexpectedly moderate performance of dyslexic children in those areas in which they are presumed to have better abilities is due to such a loss of motivation. On the other hand, psychological factors may play a part. If a child is regarded as stupid because of not being able to keep up in reading and spelling, there is a high risk of his or her achievements being inferior over the whole range of subjects.

Uncertainty, fear of failure, lack of motivation and functional or even structural regression of the areas of the brain concerned probably all contribute to the apparent intellectual falling asleep of a dyslexic child who has been neglected from an educational point of view.

On what grounds can schools refuse pupils who have been registered?

In the UK, parents have the choice of school, provided it is not full. The school is obliged to admit a child unless it has no place available or unless the child has a 'Statement of Special Educational Needs'. In the latter case, the child must attend the school named in the Statement unless the parents choose to educate the child outside the state system.

Are there schools that devote special attention to dyslexic children?

In the UK, all state schools should offer support to dyslexic children either from their own staff or from a local authority support service. In reality this support is very patchy. The few Remedial Schools for dyslexic children are all operating in the private sector.

CHAPTER 9

Were We Really So Blind at Primary School?

How is it that Dyslexia is Sometimes Discovered so Late?

There are innumerable dyslexic children who only ran up against their handicap for the first time when they were at secondary school. Seen in retrospect, there were also indications when they were at primary school. Let us put it like this: at primary school language was definitely not their strongest side.

But of course everybody has a stronger and a weaker side and that is readily accepted at school, at any rate if the two do not diverge too far from each other. So how does it come about that things sometimes go completely wrong with these children when they reach secondary school? Why all of a sudden can they no longer keep up? Is it only now that dyslexia sometimes rears its head, after having been present for years in a latent form? Does it have to do with puberty? Or does secondary education rely very much on the less developed qualities of dyslexic children?

Can one say that children who pass through primary school relatively free of problems are dyslexic to a lesser extent than their fellows who have stumbled earlier? Or do they have more means of compensating? These are questions which are perhaps partly answered in the story that Paul and his mother tell. And in so far as they are not answered we put them to specialists.

Paul (Aged 15) tells his Story

I USED TO BE JUST AS GOOD AS MY FRIEND

I was always able to keep up very well at primary school. Only with language did I have quite a lot of difficulty. My friend always used to have to help me with it. Fortunately he was very good at school. I found that the most difficult part was copying things from the blackboard. If the teacher set a task, geography or something, it would go like this: he would start to describe something and I wouldn't understand because I was still busy.

I also found dictations difficult. I would fall behind, I would forget the sense and sometimes I would simply add something I'd made up completely. For instance, I knew such and such a word, and would think: so-and-so must go in between. But sometimes that takes you completely off the rails. The further I got at primary school the harder it became.

I was good at arithmetic but frequently rather sloppy. They always said I was too careless at it. But with a little bit more time I could certainly have worked better and then I would also have made fewer mistakes from carelessness. I did try to do my best. If I got a comment about my slapdash work I would try to do it very neatly the next time. But then the comment would be: 'You're too slow'. So at any given moment you don't know where you are.

It was not until the bridging class that it really started to go wrong. I had the feeling that I was having to work very hard to keep up with everything. So on one occasion I got a 7 but the next time it was a 5. And even for that I had to spend a really long time poring over my homework. If I relaxed for a moment I was immediately punished with a clear fail mark. The work piled up more and more and I had to spend longer and longer on my homework. And yet from time to time you also want to be doing other things, watching TV for instance. Now and again I'd think: how is this possible? I used to be just as good as my friend and now the position is that he spends an hour over his homework and gets a 10 and I spend the same time and am rewarded with a 1. I couldn't understand it at all. I thought, what on earth is going on? It simply didn't seem to add up.

With maths I was able to allow myself the luxury of not doing my best from time to time, to let things ride. In biology, physics, chemistry and economics I'm good as well. If I have a test, I glance through the material and get a 7. And if I don't glance at it I still get a 6. Next year I'm allowed to choose a range of subjects, so I know what I'll go for. If I get through this year...

My parents only came to be aware of it from the first bad reports that I brought home. And also the concept of 'dyslexia' cropped up when I came up as a doubtful case in a standard dictation which was given at that school. My parents immediately arranged for me to be tested, as I was being treated homoeopathically for an allergy and they said: 'Dyslexia is more common in children with allergies. We have homoeopathic remedies for that too'.

So I was given a few little bottles of medicine and first we would wait to see how that worked. Well, my learning achievements went in fits and starts. They went up and down continually. So you couldn't really say the homoeopathy had helped me over the problems.

When I went up from form one to form two my parents asked for a discussion with the school. 'Things aren't going well. What should we do now? Should we put him into the MAVO because the HAVO is turning out to be too hard for him? What actually seems to be the problem?' There was then a discussion and the school said: 'If we know for certain that he has dyslexia we can offer him a special programme and monitor the situation until Christmas'.

Immediately after the holidays I was then tested by a psychological bureau. The test was exciting as I too thought: there's got to be something at the bottom of all this. Sometimes I would think: let's see if it'll help if I work really hard. But it made scarcely any difference. At the most one mark. And yet I didn't feel I was stupid. I got on very well with my friends and they were mostly at the highest level.

So it is therefore almost a relief to hear that you're dyslexic, as the test showed it clearly. The psychologist discussed the results with me and told me I am intelligent enough to get into pre-university education (VWO). Only I would have to work very hard for it and he said: 'We'll see whether we can compensate for it with some exercises'. So I started doing some extra work with a teacher who had been on a special training course for this. That was out of school hours. They were exercises such as drawing curves, reading and tracing with your finger over the paper. And something else, I forget what it's called ('parallelogram', perhaps? No, that's something else) which you could make all kinds of shapes with. There were triangles and rectangles and so on and there was a little book with it with shapes which you had to fit together exactly using those bits. I sometimes had difficulty in seeing just how those went, but mostly I came up with the right solutions.

That extra work really did help, I think, as before that I was getting 3s, 4s and 5s for languages. But then I got a 7 for English, and for Dutch I had a 6. Only for German did I still get a 5. So I had progressed. Also it was really great to know: OK, that's what I've got. Now I could at least learn to live with it. Otherwise you think: what on earth am I to do now?

Then we moved house and at a new school it's very difficult at first. You spend less time on your homework because you're going around with friends and so on. Otherwise you don't get to know anybody. So at the start it went really badly. And it isn't easy to improve on your marks either. With great difficulty I had just got my French up to scratch and now I was recently given another test and crashed it again. A 1! And just before that I was at the pass level...

With a test I have to feel that there's no time constraint, because once you feel time pressure you soon start to rush and skimp. You make mistakes, and if you look over your work later you don't find them. And if I make one mistake you can be as sure as eggs are eggs that I'll repeat it throughout the test. Over and over again.

The worst is getting the words drummed into me. We've worked out that I've sometimes spent eight hours learning the

words for one test. And then there's the grammar as well. Plus
the ordinary exercises which I get for word blindness. It's also
very different as between writing it down on paper and someone listening to you. My mother and I have experienced that to
our great disappointment.

It happened like this, you see: an uncle of mine was getting married and after that weekend I was to have a word practice. A hundred English words. But we had to go to the
wedding. So my mother said: 'Well, we'll practise in the car'.
We took the book with us and we practised constantly on the
way there and on the way back. Two and a half hours there and
two and a half hours back. I knew them forwards and I knew
them backwards. But next day I got a 1 for that test. Writing is
very different from reading.

After something like that I've occasionally said to myself:
Right, that's enough. But then I think to myself: Persevere a bit
longer, as later I want to go into computers. Become a program-
mer or something like that. And for that you don't need VWO.
I've already looked into that in detail: if I have my HAVO I can
go to the technical university and after a year there I can go to
the University Technical School, the UTS, then I won't have
lost a year at all.

What is more, things can only get easier for me. After all,
close reading and listening comprehension tests are quite different from an endless stack of words. So next year I can drop the
languages, except English, but I'm fairly good at that, now.
Admittedly it's difficult, but I'll shortly be getting help from
somebody so that I can catch up a bit on the languages. And if
that works I think I will be able to get through the year...

The Mother of Paul (Aged 15) tells her Story

WE FELT HE WASN'T PUTTING IN ENOUGH EFFORT

Paul didn't actually have language problems as such until
he was at secondary school. Then they became really apparent,
because his results were minimal, far below what had been

expected. You see, at primary school he was among the best pupils. But then at that stage he was still able to do everything orally. He had so much information from home that he stuck out above the average.

He got to secondary school and that was very frustrating for him: suddenly all that was gone. Everything was new and he had to learn a great deal that he didn't know anything about. He made the discovery — and this was something he said at home — that he didn't have anything more to say at school. He had suddenly gone from being a boy who said a lot to one who didn't say anything any more.

He changed too. In form one he was very frustrated and nervous. Always very tense. He looked very pale. But then one thinks: he's in a growth phase and that sort of thing. As a mother you don't always know what the problem is. But I could see that he was getting more nervous as time went on. He had stomachache too.

The whole situation was only explained by the results of that test. It showed clearly that things were escalating. Paul was falling further and further behind in the language area. And in retrospect it could have been clear a lot earlier that he was word-blind.

Once we had the outcome of that test I went back to his primary school, with his reports, and said: 'Don't you actually keep track of your children?' Because if there are phenomena which keep recurring whilst the teachers are saying: 'He's really a highly intelligent child', then surely there must be something wrong somewhere?

At that school I said to them: 'It seems that about ten per cent of all children are dyslexic. So how is it that nobody is acknowledged to be dyslexic at your school?' 'Well', they replied, 'we hate putting labels on people'. But I would say: 'it's thanks to a label that at least you know what's the matter, and how you ought to be responding to certain phenomena. And perhaps it even indicates guidelines for what you can do about it!'

Because we didn't know what the trouble was, you see, we kept Paul's nose to the grindstone when he was at primary school. So did the teachers, in fact. He was really given what for — not that he was literally hit, but we were for ever saying: 'Now do pay attention and just do your best. Don't sit there day-dreaming and make sure you get those tables learnt!' It was our impression that he wasn't putting in enough effort.

His primary school reports often said: 'Must pay attention to his spelling!' And: 'His work is too slovenly!' And another time — this is absolutely typical — it said: 'Must work faster!' I remember us saying to each other at that time: 'Now what is it they're after? Do they want him to work fast or do they want him to work neatly?'

There was one teacher in class six who hammered away at him dreadfully about his handwriting. In that class Paul would just have to write more neatly. That man was in the habit of knocking Paul on his arm while he was writing. You see, the boy always wrote in a very cramped way, holding his pen too stiffly. But the result of him being knocked was always a line across the paper. I thought that was really sadistic. What also happened was that that teacher would set a test for a particular day and at the last minute it wasn't given. Paul always revised very hard for tests like that, but if it was given without warning a week later it would be a lost cause. He couldn't retain things properly. What *was* a big advantage was that Paul is a fanatical reader. That was also mentioned in the test results: because he has read a great deal he is familiar with lots of synonyms. Also, both my husband and I were still on courses ourselves, so that meant there was plenty of professional language being bandied about, often technical terms. At the primary school they said they thought it was really odd that Paul found some things so difficult, because he always had a ready answer for everything, could always say the things people wanted to hear. He knew a great deal and needed few dictionaries. There was so much that he was able to explain.

For that reason no alarm bells ever rang as far as I was concerned. To my way of thinking Paul was coping well at school and I thought it was quite normal that he had to struggle so long with, say, tables. They'd always given me considerable trouble too. And to be honest I still don't know them very well.

I really thought that it was the same for everyone. It's not something you talk about, they're just rotten things to learn.

But it was very different with Paul's younger sister. She never needed to learn tables, she could simply do it. Paul could not, and then we said: 'You really must practise more, my lad'. We thought he wasn't doing enough. Also I hadn't been paying enough attention; there's no doubt I'm a poor mother — I find it such a business keeping track of all those things.

All the same, the time came when we started practising really fanatically. Every morning we started with the tables; this was when he was in class four of primary school. But by the time he got to class six he'd forgotten them again. So then we had to start again at the beginning. I feel really guilty about it now, when I think how we kept him on his toes!

It all applies to me too. However, I did have vague suspicions about the difficulties Paul was having at school, because it also occurs in my family. I am dyslexic as well; it was simply that I didn't know that that's what it was, I didn't have a name for it. But I do know that we all had dreadful problems with languages. In some cases the problems weren't with reading, incidentally. If we had to do a year over again that was because of language skills. My mother had to stay down in class two once if not twice at primary school. I think we have inherited it from her.

When I started reading more and more about it I thought: gosh, all this applies to me too. I recognise a great deal of myself in it and of my brother as well. My brother simply persisted. He didn't care what people said. He was regarded as stupid, because he was bad at languages, even worse than Paul. He had to go to the LTS, but he got his MAVO (lower general secondary education) and later his HAVO (higher general secondary education). With a great deal of trouble, of course. After that he got his business and economics qualifications (HEAO)* and now he's at university! So all I mean is: that isn't the cause. It isn't to do with your intelligence. But it is very frustrating, as you don't live up to your promise, you don't come into your own. In our family, for example, they're not all that skilled with their hands either. Nor is Paul; when he was small he couldn't make anything out of Lego or Fisher using a plan. He can now, of course; he can count and reason things out now.

But because you're deficient in certain areas you perhaps develop other aspects more, to compensate and to show that there really is something in you. So Paul has his computer, which he can handle really well. And my brother has been able to thoroughly prove himself in maths and economics, whilst I have tried to prove myself first by getting my MAVO for mothers and then the evening class HAVO.

Because of this recognition I do at least have a little bit of understanding for Paul. But my husband can't grasp that if you have learnt something really well it doesn't follow that you're able to reproduce it. He often says: 'You've been in your room, Paul. What have you been doing up there?' He does try to understand it, but it won't come home to him that all the tests show that Paul is sufficiently intelligent but in spite of that he doesn't succeed.

I don't go constantly looking to see what Paul is doing upstairs, mind. And also I do know he's quite likely to be reading comic strips; after all he's still only a child and he can get away with very little. But I must say I feel thoroughly guilty about all the tellings off we gave him at primary school. I intend not to take such a negative approach towards him in future, but a positive one instead. A stimulating one, in other words. If he's worked really well and is given a fail mark, well, that's a pity, there's nothing you can do about it, he's done his best.

I wish there was more evidence of understanding at his present school, but that would be asking rather a lot. I did once say to them that the time pressure on Paul when they were doing tests was such a difficult point for him. However, they couldn't see it at all, as he always finished too early. Then I said: 'It's more the idea that he has too little time and that's why he does his tests far too quickly. Checking over his work doesn't have any meaning for him. He simply needs to feel that he can spend just as much time on it as he wants'.

Because he does need a lot of time. Then he quietly analyses each sentence and applies all the available formulae. As long as he can reason it out, you see, he's a lot further on. He thinks up all kinds of mnemonics and little wrinkles to camouflage his handicap. That's something I've always done too. In that way you learn to live with it: you adapt. It's simply that some things remain which are more time and trouble.

The amusing thing is that now I know both Paul and I are dyslexic I discover so many correspondences with the child. It really has given us a good bond. We often have to laugh at our both making the same mistakes. Take the word 'interest', for instance. It's only now that I know how to write it. I've always written 'intrest', but it seems you have to put an 'e' in somewhere.

Recording words in your mind, it turns out, is something we just don't do very well. You might have read a word hundreds of times in books but you've never noticed how you're to write it. You don't stop and ponder over it at all. In addition, whilst we're practising Paul and I come across really crazy things. For instance he didn't know the word 'huge'. With him it was always 'big' or 'large'. And instead of 'town hall' he would always say something like 'mayor's house'.

With learning a series of things Paul and I always have to give our complete attention. They always have to be learnt in random sequence, never in the same order, or else all you know is that if you have a word with two t's then it's followed by a word with one 't'. But if you learn it like that the word doesn't say anything to you, you don't recognise anything in it.

Other correspondences we have discovered are our problems with left and right. Putting out your hand in the traffic, that's something Paul has also long had difficulty with. And he also has a problem with time. He would always turn up late, he didn't have any sense of time. It isn't so bad now he has a watch. I think you have to acquire a certain rhythm if you want to learn to cope with it. If he doesn't have any order he's lost.

Everyone has his peculiarities, of course, and over time you find ways of learning to live with them. You can also ask yourself: when does a peculiarity become a handicap? In Paul's case it only really became so at secondary school, with his

dyslexia. Or were we so blind when he was at primary school?
Ought we to have picked it up earlier?

Commentary by Specialists

SECONDARY SCHOOLS ALSO NEED TO BE ALERT TO THE POSSIBLE EXISTENCE OF READING AND SPELLING PROBLEMS

Chapter 1 covered the aspect that primary schools attach less importance nowadays than they used to do to the technical aspects of reading and writing. At most primary schools attention has been transferred to the aspects of language teaching which concern content, such as speaking skills and the ability to express oneself in writing. On the one hand we should not be surprised that in secondary education more pupils are being encountered who are backward in reading and writing, and on the other hand this makes it possible to understand how it is that pupils who have not got reading and spelling completely under their belts often slip through primary school unnoticed. They have not yet had the spotlight shine on them, especially if they have the ability to compensate in the form of gifts to which the primary school attaches more importance.

At secondary school — Chapter 8 showed this — there is renewed reliance on the pupil's reading and spelling capabilities. And both the dyslexic child as well as children with arrears of teaching in the areas of reading and spelling will then be shocked to discover that they are unable to cope. So it is that secondary education is burdened with a not inconsiderable number of pupils who for these reasons cannot process the material being taught. Are these pupils then all to fall by the wayside? Must a great accumulation of talent remain unexploited because the link between primary education and secondary education isn't a perfect fit?

Although in practice there does not seem to be too much understanding of the specific problems which a large number of children in bridging classes have to struggle with, a number of simple measures could in themselves avoid a great number of difficulties. These measures have to do first and foremost with teaching and relate to the fact that most problem pupils simply do not know what they are supposed to do with the material being taught them. To start with such pupils need to be taught how to study. And there are ways of doing this. For example one can pay attention to the applicability of what is being taught. It must be made clear to pupils that learning is not a matter of merely having things drummed into you, but that the material (hopefully) consists of meaningful connections.

In this context it is also worth pointing out that when pupils are being assessed it is not enough just to go by 'the answer' or 'the result'. This one-sided concentration on results is the reason why pupils attach less importance to reasoning things out, to the thinking process that leads to the answer. At the same time, with a little thought a great deal of rote-learning at secondary school could be avoided.

In addition, recurring mistakes for which pupils are reprimanded will sap their motivation, which will also suffer if specific progress is not reflected in the marks awarded. If you get a mark of 1 for having 50 mistakes in your dictation test and the same mark for making 15 mistakes, that will tend to make you give up. It would be better if pupils were taught how to check and correct their own written work. That is a much more meaningful way of showing them their mistakes. The modifications above all have to do with teaching, and would also benefit pupils who do not have learning problems. However, there are other more specific measures that can be taken to do justice to pupils with reading and spelling problems. In this connexion one needs to bear in mind that everything that a pupil with problems has to do in writing means a greater burden for him or her. This can be catered for either by making more time available for written tests or from time to time skipping over the written evidence of pupils' written attainments by giving more oral tests, not dictating too much, writing the homework up in a box on the blackboard at the beginning of the lesson, handing out duplicated sheets and so on. In addition the use of dictionaries, typewriters and tape recorders could be tolerated or even

encouraged. Provided the pupil has already used these aids at
school for some time, they could also be accepted for external
examinations such as GCSE or 'A' levels. Extended time may
be offered by examination boards if requests are made in good
time and usually supported by a recommendation from an educational psychologist.

QUESTIONS

*Can you require from dyslexic children at secondary school
that they should be able to write without errors, or as a teacher
should you pay no attention at all to the mistakes in their
written work?*

It is always hard to find the right balance between understanding the handicap and the requirements that must still be
placed on a child. In addition there may be a variation from
pupil to pupil. What is certain is that demands can and must be
made on dyslexic pupils, even in the area of their handicap. It
may be that they will never learn to write without any mistakes
at all, but they must be made fully aware of the deficiency and
as far as possible must make an effort to confine the harm within certain limits. At any rate they must write in a legible way.
They must be able to put clearly into writing what they mean.
The next step is for them to find and correct their mistakes, or
at least make an effort in that direction.

So it is permissible to require that dyslexic pupils should
take steps forward, so long as one does not ask the impossible
of them, so long as they are not confronted by a mountain that
completely blocks their path. Nor need the situation ever reach
that stage so long as side by side with those demands one also
shows plenty of understanding — understanding of what it
means to have such difficulty in grasping written language.
That understanding also means that one will not straight away
blame a possible failure or setback on a lack of will, lack of
concentration or idiocy. Unless the contrary is shown, the
dyslexic pupil is doing his or her best. Their achievements will
proceed in fits and starts and it therefore makes a lot of sense to

praise progress as highly as possible and not to put too much stress on steps backward, as that will be discouraging.

Does dyslexia also have implications for areas other than languages?

All subjects which involve reading and/or writing are potential stumbling blocks for dyslexic pupils. However, the languages are clearly the biggest barrier. Depending on the teacher and the approach used, subjects like geography and history can be a source of certain difficulties. In particular, teachers who include writing mistakes in their assessments make it impossible for dyslexic children to be given their due in those subjects. Even maths, chemistry and physics can suffer from the handicap. The problem here is mainly that the child does not read the question properly. It can therefore do no harm to get a pupil used to reading the question through twice. Also, in the case of a wrong answer one needs to ask oneself whether the answer given fits a rather different question.

In general one could say that the problems could remain restricted to the languages if the teachers of the other subjects could bring some understanding to it. Unfortunately this is by no means always the case.

CHAPTER 10

And They Call That Dyslexic!

Can you be Dyslexic and yet go to University?

The previous chapters show that for most children who are burdened by it dyslexia forms a significant barrier to their getting through their school careers smoothly. Often what is in them does not come out, or by means of all manner of detours parents try to see that their children take their rightful place. It is perfectly understandable that the various aspects will be accompanied by a number of frustrations, and it is a very general shortcoming that as a result the difficulties will extend far beyond the limits of the original problem. Dyslexia, as all the stories show, is an invisible handicap; this is true, but perhaps precisely because of that it has very many implications.

Jurgen (aged 25) doesn't agree with that at all. He has managed to restrict the problem to a number of isolated school subjects and otherwise has refused to be discouraged. After achieving a splendid result in his school-leaving certificate he went off to university. His dyslexia has not gone away but it plays a relatively subordinate role. And Jurgen is trying to keep it like that. 'You have to accept that you're less strong in certain areas', he says, 'but that does not mean that you therefore have to give in to it'.

Has Jurgen simply been lucky? Have things not been made so hard for him in his school life as for most children who are dyslexic? Or have other factors also played a part in his having emerged from the struggle without damage? Was the fact of his dyslexia perhaps not a handicap in his case?

In this chapter we will perhaps come to know more about dyslexia as it affects the highly gifted.

Jurgen (Aged 25) tells his Story

WHEN YOU'RE A BIG BOY YOU LEARN TO READ

When I was at infants' school I was always busy with numbers and with my hands. It was very clear that I was ahead of the rest of the children. But at primary school it soon became obvious that I was going to have difficulty. Even at that early stage I had already used a typewriter, but then I was just copying character by character. That had nothing to do with reading or writing.

I didn't have the slightest urge to understand letters. Everyone always read to me. When we got the first reading book — I can still remember that well — I therefore thought: ah, great, reading aloud, looking at nice pictures! But it turned out that we had to do it ourselves and I remember that that gave me a real shock. I had thought it would be a few years before that stage was reached; when you're a big boy you learn to read.

We didn't use the spelling method of reading but an American method. This involved learning the word as a whole, so you didn't learn J/A/M/E/S, but James. You had to recognise that image. So what I did was this. I simply learnt the sequence of those letters by heart, without attaching much significance to them. I did know that the 'h' was an 'h' but it was only years later that I grasped how everything actually fitted together.

When I was in class three at primary school we moved house and I found myself at a Montessori school. There it was crystal clear that I was rather backward as far as reading and writing were concerned. And it was only there that they taught me what the situation was with double 'l's and suchlike. At least it was only then that it got through to me.

At the previous school, a village school, I'd been able to get by reasonably well. Of course, learning all those words by heart is one way of doing things. But it doesn't give you a very big vocabulary. You need to have seen each word once. You can't just write something down from its sound. That does make it extremely arduous.

At that time my parents noticed that I read very little compared to my sister. She more or less worked her way right through the book-case when she was in class three. She reads in a sloping way, from top left to bottom right. She scans the page. To my way of thinking she leafs through whole books like that, whilst if I have to read a book I still find it terribly hard work.

My parents tried very hard to push me with all sorts of little books. I'd absolutely no inclination for it — they were all those old-fashioned reading primers. But I did start reading lots of cartoon strips. Of course they don't make you very much wiser, though eventually I became an ace at recognising such words as BIFF, SMASH and UGH.

Everybody in the class read real books, children's books, but I had an enormous resistance to reading them. The only things I read apart from comic strips were encyclopaedias and things like that. Never the text, but above all the illustrations and the captions to them. I also tended to cut the photographs out of everything. The story wasn't so important, it was the photograph that was of much greater interest. As far as writing is concerned, in those first years at primary school, I believe, the emphasis was mainly on how you wrote rather than what you wrote. It was nearly all copying. I didn't reverse the 'p's and so on but for years I spelt a word like 'hand' wrongly. I mixed all the letters up. The 'h' and 'd' were often in the right place but what came in between was pure chance. For a while it was h, n, a, d. And 'career', I still can't write that. At any rate I always have to think carefully about it. You think that it's c, r, e e, r or something like that. I always get that completely mixed up.

So at the Montessori school it was very clear that I was tremendously behind in reading and spelling. But I was ahead, or at any rate good, at arithmetic, geography and general knowledge. So basically I didn't have all that many problems — it was simply a nuisance, especially dictations, which were always hell. At the start things were still going well, but from class three onwards there were real problems. Then I could no longer cope and got really poor marks.

I did get some extra lessons from teachers but they never put me in the dunce's corner. That was the only thing I had difficulty with. And I had such a ready tongue, of course. It was absolutely clear that the problem lay in reading and writing.

I really don't know how it all started, because of course you could say that I just have an aversion to reading. For a long time I also resisted learning to spell. In fact that's true of me still: it's boring. If you say 'dyslexia' you straight away think of something that's inherent, in my nervous system. But with me it's like this: perhaps I have no inclination for it. But it's also very clear that for me it goes against the grain. Being able to spell properly is simply of no interest to me.

But I do read a lot. It was only very late on that I started reading. Popular scientific books, periodicals such as '*LOOK*' and aircraft books. At some stage when I was at secondary school or at the end of primary school I started reading the newspaper. And I found that interesting. It was something new every day. Books were not interesting as I tended to read a book that I knew three times. I didn't have the need to start on a different book that was unknown to me. All those pages, that put me off.

But through the newspaper, a provincial, easily-digested one, I started to read every day. And then my reading speed did go up. Also there were lots of illustrations in the semi-scientific material I was reading. I still find it frightening to read a book without illustrations. Whilst reading I often say to myself: when do I get to the next picture?

At the end of primary school of course I was given a Cito test*, but spelling only formed a minor part of it. Parsing sentences, for instance — I was very good at that, it was water off a duck's back to me. It was simply a matter of applying a number of simple rules, a thoroughly logical whole. Language is not really logical, it crawls with exceptions. I'm not really clear about the difference between 'c' and 'k' for instance. 'Sceptical' — no, that doesn't start with a 'c', it starts with an 'S'. But what about 'September'?

In the Cito test I came out in the top percentile. General knowledge 99 or thereabouts. Arithmetic around 94. And language — yes, I was behind in that with a 68. That again shows that it's really a relative problem. There were children in the class whose spelling was worse than mine but they were behind in everything. It may well be that overall I still spell better than the average Dutch person! And they call that dyslexic?

LOTS OF CRIBBING

The first dictation at secondary school was still all right: I got a 7. But after that I only got 1s, and the dictations got more and more difficult. I couldn't hold my own. I often changed whole pieces in those dictations. For instance if the teacher said 'progressive', a word that I really couldn't write, I would make it into 'left-wing'. Often when he marked it he simply skipped over it. All the same I still had 50 mistakes, so that was a −40! That was pointless. I knew in advance that I couldn't do dictations all that well. Nevertheless I was given a 1.

But at the start I was able to compensate with other things. Even the languages still went OK in form one. It was simply a matter of working very hard and I still had the spirit to do that. Generally the material was conveniently set out. For a test it was always chapters 3 to 6 or something like that. That was something you could learn by heart. For French and English I was perhaps spending twenty per cent of the time learning material for tests. The rest of the time I was drumming words into myself, not seeking the correct translation — I quickly grasped how to do that — but to get the letters of the words in the right order! Sometimes that took me whole nights. Then I had to keep redoing it all the time. It was simply a matter of drumming it in, sticking it into your memory. I had absolutely no system. At the end of the day a language will then always be completely foreign to you.

In form two German was added and my sisters had already told me it was horrible and the teachers would all be ghastly. Well, that's just how it was! It was a real stereotype. So then I had three languages to do. I got through the second year with them, the third... But in the fourth year they came to a grinding halt. The whole thing went to pot. On my final report I had an 8 for maths, an 8 for biology, a 1 for German, a 2 for French and a 3 for English! My average was still six but you can see the problem.

There were all sorts of adolescent factors as well — I was a punk for a while and simply could no longer get myself to work so hard at something that interested me so little and in which I could see so little point. Of course I very much wanted to learn a language. I still want to learn to speak French well. But the fact that I had to get down to learning to spell all those words... I could see no purpose in it at all. If I go to France I want to be able to speak French. Surely I won't be required to draft a letter in French?

So my motivation was wholly lacking. I was blowed if I was going to learn the past historic when you knew before you started that you'd never speak it. In form four it was soon clear that I wouldn't be able to set things to rights so I didn't go up.

The second time round I got through, though with great difficulty. I worked terribly hard. I was so dreadfully behind! Writing essays, for example, I couldn't do that at all. And German. That was excruciating! *Wort und Satz*, a little green book, you needed literally to know the whole thing off pat. Oh, how I hated that! I would stomp up and down my bedroom in impatience! In itself working hard is very enjoyable, but this was so meaningless, learning a sentence off by heart when you know it relates to nothing at all. You never use sentences like that, you do it purely and simply for the school, just to get that mark.

Of course I tried as hard as I could to get round my foreign language spelling problems, by learning things completely by heart or by getting marks in oral exercises. Usually in written work I would have all the letters of a word there. I always knew approximately how long the word was, so the first few letters were right and also the last few, the ending. I'd gradually managed to discover a system for that. But what came in between was always a shambles.

Finally I went up to the next form with a 6 in English — the English teacher had given me a bit of a helping hand — a 3 or 4 for German and a 5 for French. And then I was able to drop German and French! I still had to do English. I didn't know quite how I was going to do that as at that stage I still couldn't read a single letter of English. From time to time I'd bought things about aeroplanes, an English magazine. I started off with it very bravely, using a dictionary, but when you have to look up every word...

In form five English quickly became more difficult. Each new fact submerged the previous one. Most of my classmates were already reading English books and magazines — I had the feeling that it was something that just seemed to waft over them. And I must admit I got through form five with a lot of cribbing, as you were allowed to have only one 5 on your final list and that was an unattainable figure for my English.

Finally we had a central test, a leaving examination held two or three years ago. It's true that that was marked rather more generously than the one in form six, but all the same... I then tried to get hold of all the answers for the last few years, but when we were examined it turned out to be a state exam, one that I didn't have, so my cribs were no use to me.

It was no easy task, because at that time I was an easy fail in English. But I had a terrifically lucky break as next to me there was a friend of mine who was fantastic at English. His mother was an English teacher and it was all as easy as pie for him. He never needed to take any trouble over it.

In front of the class there was a geography teacher reading a book. So with my palms sweating I copied everything from my friend, as I didn't know what the text was about. I hadn't the slightest idea! Also I was so nervous that I scarcely made any attempt. But to create the impression that I was working I sat hunched over the text. For each block I put about two extra mistakes in. Otherwise it would have been too noticeable. And so I went up from form five to form six.

LEAVING EXAM

Form six was enjoyable, as other aspects of the language were also highlighted. Also I then started reading books, for Dutch. Of course for the most part they were books which weren't all that difficult. So to some extent you get the hang of it. I got a 9 for my oral. I also passed easily on my talk. For reading aloud I had a 5, I think, but that only counts for a twelfth of the total mark. Command of the language — comprehension tests, those were a piece of cake. It was all multiple choice. I'm a great fan of multiple choice, of course.

In form six I devoted an enormous amount of attention to that book list and to essays and making extracts. I read a terrific number of extracts, because you can buy books which contain sample leaving exam questions in them. In particular I paid attention to how the system operated, what they asked and how you had to read the texts. That paid off in the final exams; the extracts went fine, except that the usual marks had to come off for my spelling.

The essay went well too. Of course I knew in advance that they would set a current affairs topic. Squatting, or extra-parliamentary demos, they were bound to have something about that. So I'd already written a piece on that, and I'd learnt all the difficult words in it by heart. My English letter — well, of course, that was written out in my dictionary, so at least I couldn't make any mistakes in that. Fortunately you're allowed to take your own dictionary into the final exams. Of course you need an introduction and an end for each letter. In my case those were pretty long and there was scarcely anything in between. Of course it isn't quite right, it's a bit dodgy but that's how I managed to get through that as well.

But the biggest stumbling block was the English text. In form six I would have to do a similar test to the one in form five, in which I'd had to copy everything because I didn't know what it was about. And I was really afraid of that. Then in that year I started reading English strip cartoons like crazy, and technical books and even pornography. As long as it grabbed my attention. Because real literature — I couldn't get into that. However beautiful or artistic it might be I simply didn't give my attention to it. Perhaps I just wasn't so sensitive to that kind of nuance. At any rate I needed to have something I could enjoyably bash through, something that would give me a bit of practice.

For the English book list I even set to work with the library for the blind. Using the cassette tapes at least you then had the story, and that was important for the leaving exams.

And in addition as preparation for the examinations I made a serious study of the multiple choice system, how the questions are derived from the texts. I sussed it out: out of the four answers there is often a very long one. It's hardly ever that one. One is very short, and you can bet your boots that isn't the right one either. And then there are two about the same length. Those are the ones you have to choose between. So you can score more than evens merely by the length of the answers.

And also there is often an answer with words which are taken almost literally from the text. Now that isn't the one either. There is then often something reversed, there will be a 'not' somewhere in between the words or something like that. At any rate there is a system to it — the most important thing is that you should seek out the two answers that are important. You then have to weigh those two against each other. If you again compare with the text, you'll be successful. And I then got a 9.3 for that, a really incredible mark!

I also knew exactly how much time I could spend on each section. I had the clock next to me and if I had gone past the time allowed I merely went on to the next text. I had also built in some extra time, and so at the end I was able to correct the parts where it had all gone wrong. I worked myself to death for three hours, with that 9.3 as the result. So the system got its own back for my cribbing in form five!

With that 9.3 I was also able to make up for the English letter, as in spite of my precautions that was riddled with mistakes of course. So on my final list I eventually had a 7 for English or perhaps even an 8. At any rate the language-type subjects had come on enormously but the science subjects were still rather marking time. They were not fails, of course, but they were 7s and so on. I had plenty of understanding of them but the practice was lacking, and so was a big slice of readily available knowledge.

I'M NO SLOUCH IN EXAMS

So in that final year at secondary school maths and the science subjects had completely passed me by. I had put so much effort into Dutch and English that chemistry, physics and maths had rather gone by the board. It was when there were tests that I always rediscovered how things were going. And it was really crazy, as when I had prepared really badly for a test I was always in the top band, but if I'd prepared thoroughly I always came somewhere in the middle.

At any rate when I started studying chemistry at university I soon realised I was way behind. Then they said: 'Calculate an equilibrium', and although I knew the principle perfectly well, before I had worked it all out those guys had already done it, working it out roughly. After a fortnight at university I could already see that I would have to put in stacks of time to catch up. And I'd been looking forward so much to the freedom of student life…

Another aspect was that I'd really wanted to go and study psychology. In form five I'd read a book by Freud — well, the first 60 pages of it, but for me that was quite a lot! That man writes fantastically, it's really ridiculous. He's so convinced that he's in the right! And it's all so anecdotal, lovely stories about people. At that time I wrote an essay about how Freud had arrived at his theories, and that is how I became interested in psychology.

However, I was advised on all sides not to study psychology. People said you had to read an enormous number of books in English for it, so I thought I'd better not do that. But then I thought the chemistry was going badly, so I felt that if I have to devote so much time to studying, it would be better if I did something I enjoyed. And so after only two weeks I arranged to be transferred to psychology.

Those English books were indeed a disaster! The very first page I had to read…I think it took me an hour. And at the end of the hour I was a complete wreck. But then one day I got hold of an extract from that book in Dutch, and that helped greatly, as up to then I had felt just like a Chinese — sitting

there staring at every word without the slightest inkling whether
it is significant. What I mean is: it makes no odds whether it's
a reference or a footnote, you still have to look everything up.

All the same, there comes a time when you at least get
hold of the words commonly used in psychology — and a book
of that kind definitely uses a certain jargon. So the day came
when I was up to three pages an hour. Then at least there's
something happening in the hour; at the very least you can turn
the page twice! And little by little I saw an improvement. Now
I'm up to five pages an hour, and every picture in the book
improves my average.

There is one advantage: although I read very slowly everything I read goes in immediately. For an exam I read a book
through once, then perhaps I read the summary again or learn a
series of topics by heart and look at a number of key words.

I've become aware that people who read very fast often
have to read the material twice, whereas after reading something once I can often call to mind whole passages from a book.
My father, for instance; he reads a great deal and very fast but
afterwards he can only remember the general atmosphere of a
book. What he retains is in rather poetical terms: a rainy, foggy
or sunny book — that sort of description. Perhaps because he
reads much more than I do he doesn't remember every book
exactly.

At any rate at the end of the day I think I prepare for an
exam just as quickly as anybody else. I'm now a sixth year student and have a year to go. As an option I have chosen psy-
chonomy/psychophysiology. I want to go down the research
avenue; that's congenial to me. I enjoy messing about with
computers. If I'm working with computers I still very often get
rubbish back because I've keyed a word in wrongly. 'Syntax
error' and 'undeclared identifier', that's the sort of thing you
get raining down on you. For instance I often write 'Right line'
with a 'W'. Still, that sort of thing can easily be corrected.

I don't have to think to type a text out properly, as my girlfriend does it for me. There's no sense at all in my doing typing
because I type wrong words which I read over without noticing.
Some people then pick words out of it which I would never

have dreamt were wrong. You might think those would be the really difficult words, but that's not so at all! It's precisely those words you haven't thought about at all, the words you write down without considering, automatically. Time and time again I've also written my own name down wrongly. I couldn't write my name until class three at primary school.

So I am still bothered by the dyslexia, but not excessively so. For instance I had a troublesome supervisor, a neuropsychologist. He paid lots of attention to errors, but fortunately I was often able to dictate my reports on patients onto tape and then the secretary typed them up. But if I'd ever done it myself he would have laughed me out of court. He didn't take me seriously at all.

I've noticed also that if you don't spell correctly it's very hard to be taken seriously. I can well imagine that, because I myself find it difficult to take seriously somebody with a Limburg accent, or somebody who speaks disjointedly. That's just something you have to put up with. Sometimes I explain the problem in advance to people, but it isn't something you can take away from them. Sometimes I say I'm dyslexic but I often hesitate to call it that. You see, I feel that this whole dyslexia thing is a bit of a fashionable phenomenon.

From time to time I also think: if you're going to resist your own inclinations and the school system then everything will go spectacularly wrong. I myself have an almost neurotic respect for authority — to stay in the world of psychology for a moment. I was always dead scared of teachers and that makes you do your utmost to meet the demands placed on you.

On the other hand I've always tried to manipulate the system. With me, therefore, it wasn't a question of acquiring a good mastery of language but of getting through some test or other, and I'm still an ace at passing exams, in other words at doing exactly what is expected of me. It doesn't make any difference what kind of exam you stick me in front of, I'll make something out of it. And with multiple choice I always score above expectations.

At the moment I am expected to be able to produce a properly structured piece of work from my pen, and with the help of my girlfriend I'm able to do that outstandingly well. She types it and takes out all the wrong expressions I seem to use. I was always going on about 'meads and persons' and it turned out that needed to be 'Medes and Persians'.

There is also the point that when I read aloud I skip over whole sections of text. I have a sort of image in my mind which is not corrected by the text I am reading. When I'm reading I frequently think: how ridiculous, this doesn't refer to anything at all, it doesn't add up. It says exactly the opposite of what has just been stated. Then I leaf back through the book and it transpires that somewhere they *have* denied it. And that's the bit I've simply read past. What I do think is this: dyslexia must never be allowed to become an excuse for no longer doing anything about things. You may well be poor at languages but you can always improve. And it's undeniably a dreadful thing, though perhaps simply because the word does actually exist. But to go as far as to say: it's a disease... Well, I really wouldn't know what neurological structure you're supposed to imagine for it. I simply put it down to the confrontation of a certain personality with the requirements society places on it. And in particular I put it down to schools.

They also do say that dyslexia is caused by seeing everything spatially, so that you can't conceive of a word two-dimensionally. There may be something in that. For example I can't draw either. I have a hatred of making something flat that actually has space. I feel a sort of resistance to that. And nor can I properly imagine how you can convert something like sound into writing.

Reading I find interesting for the information. Of course you can also turn to the television for information, but the flow of information is too slow for me. You get no more from the TV news than you do from the front page of a newspaper. To get that information I like reading scientific articles, not novels. But reading books that only have text in them, that frightens me dreadfully! Page after page without illustrations — terrible! That still gives me an awful amount of trouble. The same with the newspaper on Saturday, masses of text and long articles. Just the thought of starting at the top left and having to struggle through the whole thing...

Commentary by Specialists

DYSLEXIA IS A RELATIVE HANDICAP

There are two things which need to be distinguished in relation to dyslexia, although they ultimately turn out to be connected. Firstly there is the fact that, as we have already discussed in Chapter 6, dyslexia is characterised by an uneven distribution of talents. That is: a dyslexic child is better at performing spatial and visual tasks than in successfully accomplishing verbal ones. Time after time these aspects are highlighted by intelligence tests.

A completely different aspect, however, is the disadvantage that a child experiences as a result of this specific aptitude profile. This disadvantage is formed by the demands imposed, and in general these match what is expected from an average child. So if dyslexic children achieve below the average level in their weakest area, language, then the fact that they are dyslexic will be regarded as an appreciable handicap, in spite of the fact that they are able to achieve above-average performance in non-language subjects.

But dyslexic children can also be so generously endowed with talents that even in their weak area, language, they can be some way above the average level. Children like that need not fall through the net as long as *average* requirements are placed on their language skills. In these cases the dyslexic distribution of talent will only become a problem if on the basis of their intelligence they opt for a school system which applies higher standards. At that moment they will need to open all the avenues of their intelligence and creativity in order to hold their own. They will then be just as handicapped as their somewhat less talented companions at primary school.

Dyslexia is therefore in fact a relative handicap. It occurs at all levels of intellectual functioning, from 'average', to 'very gifted', and probably also in the case of below-average children, but there it is less noticeable. The very intelligent dyslexic child features less in this book, because those concerned often manage to save the day extremely well. They do experience difficulties, but otherwise everything is in their favour. At primary school they would be able to forge ahead without being hindered by their handicap to any extent worth mentioning. At secondary school their ascendancy and self-confidence will also take them a long way, and around the time there is a danger of their sticking fast the end is generally in sight, so that they are still able to keep going for as long as it takes. Because they are successful in structuring and objectivising their own learning behaviour remedial help is not always necessary. Even at university they can benefit from the learning habits they have applied early on.

In this sense too, then, the handicap is a relative one. Those who have got over the 'stalemate' stage will later perhaps find that they can turn the problem to good account. First, though, most dyslexic children have to negotiate the enormous sea of troubles of their school careers. Only when these have been duly overcome can they perhaps breathe more freely.

QUESTIONS

Is it possible to be given an extension of the time allowed for examinations, including university exams?

Extended time may be offered by examination boards if requests are made in good time and usually supported by a recommendation from an educational psychologist.

Is dyslexia a fashionable phenomenon?

Although there has undeniably been rather more interest in dyslexia recently it is incorrect to refer to it in terms of a 'passing fad', as for most dyslexic people dyslexia is a serious and stubborn handicap which can have radical consequences for their social functioning! Sometimes it will completely rule their lives.

Some of these unpleasant consequences, moreover, are caused by a lack of understanding which dyslexic people are continually running up against. In the light of the ignorance which prevails amongst, for example, teachers regarding this subject it is therefore good that little by little rather more attention is being paid to this handicap. It is to be hoped that more knowledge about the phenomenon will also lead to a greater understanding of it.

CHAPTER 11

Society Does Not Give Us Our Just Deserts!

What Effects does Dyslexia Continue to have on you as an Adult?

Is dyslexia a phenomenon which finishes as soon as the school doors shut behind the interminably-teased dyslexic child? Or are you saddled with it all your life? What specific problems can dyslexia cause adults?

These are questions which in general it is perhaps very hard to answer, simply because not enough is yet known about dyslexia in adults. What is certain is that every adult carries his youthful experiences with him, not only in a psychological sense but also in the form of, for example, exam qualifications, or in the case of dyslexic people often a lack of qualifications. And qualifications are an indispensable item in our society. Hence the story which Marga now tells consists partly of an indictment of our society which, by working so rigidly, does not offer adult opportunities to adult dyslexics. As we read between the lines, Marga makes us very well aware that a youth characterised by failure and struggle continues to affect you when you are an adult.

Marga (Aged 38) tells her Story

I WAS SIMPLY BORED STIFF AT SCHOOL

It became clear in class one at primary school that I was word-blind: I was tested by a lady who evidently knew a great deal about it. She also gave me therapy. I can remember having speech training, and lots of practice at home. After two or three weeks I started to grasp it, but real reading, recognising words and so on, I did not manage until class three, and in fact I still cannot read well. I very much want to but my interest evaporates. It takes too long.

When reading started to go a little more smoothly there came a time when the therapy stopped. The idea was that as a child you then had to develop it and learn to live with the handicap. You even have cases, I've heard, which can be cured. As a result of a combination of circumstances there is then a period in which children need a push and then they pick it up.

But in my case the problem did not pass. Then as a young child you're completely dependent on the understanding which this person or that can bring to your peculiarity. Sometimes teachers at school were people of good will, but they couldn't make exceptions, after all, so you are continually banging your head against a brick wall. How it is coped with at home is then enormously important. My mother has always backed me to the hilt. She consoled me when I was having difficulties and inspired me with fresh courage.

Until class three I always went up on a conditional basis. My biggest problem was that I was put into the dunce's corner. I was for ever being told off and was the laughing-stock of the class. Turns at reading aloud were a disaster and eventually the time came when I was just passed over. We were still learning to write using dip pens and inkpots and if you had so many satisfactory marks for writing you were allowed to use a fountain pen. That was in class four, I think. But of course I was below that level the whole time. Well, then I really threw in the towel! I'm quite a spitfire and my self-control evaporated completely. In fact I was bored to death at school. But the marks were so important! Arithmetic was never a problem and nor were geography or history. But I was repeatedly running up against the problem that everything was assessed on your ability with words. Even with geography and history all your writing mistakes are taken into account, so time and again I was given very bad reports.

The dictations were a particularly weak area. One might as well forget trying to make them into anything decent! What are you to do? As you're supposed to, you write it down. You don't have the slightest idea what a word looks like; that's something I still can't do. I write as I hear it and as I think it ought to be written. But to anybody else it might as well say abracadabra. And usually even I can't read it back.

Sometimes with dictations I was absolutely convinced that I'd done them properly. I read it over a hundred times and thought it looked good. But then I would get it back and there wasn't a single word that was right. The crazy thing is that you can't at that moment see where you've gone wrong. Sometimes if you put it aside for three or four weeks and then examine it again you think to yourself: how could I possibly have written that? How could I have been so stupid?

Another thing with me: my thoughts were often much further ahead than the material I was working on at that particular moment, so in essays I would sometimes miss out whole words and sentences. And there again, you can read it over but you just don't notice it.

Ultimately I didn't do well enough to go up from class four. Something like that just happens to you, and you go along with it. Because it was discovered so early there was also understanding at home. It was just at school that people weren't receptive to it, as although the tests showed clearly that I was a typical gymnasium child as far as the sciences were concerned, that never came out. People never had an eye for that.

I did have one master who marked my dictations differently. Where previously I received a 2 if there were ten mistakes, I now got a 7. And also in class five I had a teacher who, though she didn't know what dyslexia was, was open to it. She gave me extra lessons. But the lack of understanding remained. Then they say: 'They ought to be able to do this, they ought to be able to do that...', and I really couldn't. The time comes when you do indeed develop complexes and become frustrated and desperate.

So it was that with great difficulty I got through primary school. I failed the admission exam twice. After the first time I came home and said: 'I've failed'. Nobody believed me, as at that time I was an average pupil. The head teacher himself said: 'If you've failed, so will the rest of the class'. Well, of the 220 who took the exam there was one failure and that was me.

The day came — I'll never forget it — when the letter was delivered at home. There it was and my mother was out walking the dog. Now something we never did and which it never crossed our minds to do was to open the post. But at that moment I tore open the envelope. I saw that I had failed and went off to school perfectly calmly, where in the playground I asked: 'Have you heard anything?' 'No'. 'Well, I've failed'. I said that as cool as you please but until that letter arrived I had secretly cherished some hope. And the moment everybody knew, the tension in me was released and I was in tears.

It was decided that I should do class six over again, but I couldn't face it and ultimately I went into advanced primary education (ULO)*. I was about 13. I stuck with that for less than three months, as I had to learn all sorts of tables and lists by heart and I couldn't do that. I couldn't cope with that system. If I can see logic, OK — but blindly learning something off by heart... Until the admission exam I was then in an IVO or seventh class. Then the admission exam again — again I failed. And finally I ended up at a sort of experimental MULO.

I'VE NEVER REALLY LEARNT TO STUDY

Things went well at that MULO. To my way of thinking I was an ordinary average pupil. But I didn't go up from form one because of my languages: English, French and Dutch. I could speak them all well but couldn't write a single word!

In year two I was more out of the class than in it. If there was something going on in the class I was thrown out, whether or not I had anything to do with it. That's something I suffer from still: nobody ever believes me, nobody takes me seriously.

Of course I was bored in that class, but I was terrifically conscientious. As far as that goes I was a model pupil. I did create if they sent me out, but once you have a bad name it's impossible to shake it off. They wanted me to do that second year again... A fierce discussion then took place and under pressure from my mother they let me go up. It turned out that I had a report showing 2s, 3s and 4s for my languages and 9s for all my other subjects! But if you have one 4 you have to stay down. It's bureaucracy gone mad: they can't make any exceptions.

All the same I went into form two and I don't know whether it was in form two or three that I had to stay down again. At any rate a time came when I was unbearable at school and unbearable at home. Then my mother said: 'Things can't go on like this. The whole family's being affected'. And I was tested again, which once more showed that I had a pronounced aptitude for the sciences. I was simply not at home at that MULO.

My mother then went to talk to the headmaster of a comprehensive school (Rijksscholengemeenschap)* in the neighbourhood. He was the first person we found who had an understanding of the whole situation. He was very interested and said: 'Whatever the problem is, she must come to school here. The question is only how best we can cope with her together'.

They sent me on a special homework course. There I spent two and a half months on algebra, geometry, chemistry and physics, as although I had an aptitude for them I had fallen a long way behind at the MULO. Physics and geometry I'd never had. Algebra I'd been taught for a year at a very low level. Also I spent whole days practising languages, just writing them.

I went there in November and was to stay until the end of the school year. But after those two and a half months I ran away screaming. That man was so awfully strict! You were handled like a child who refused to work. And of course that approach didn't work with me at all.

Finally I went as a 'supernumerary'* at that school's community. I would use the summer holiday to make up the backlog. I'd already caught up on chemistry in those two and a half months and for algebra and geometry I worked in the corridor. After school hours I was also given extra maths lessons.

For the first time in my life I then really had to work. I can tell you, I was a totally different person! I got home at half-past-four and then still had to do my homework and also homework for the extra lessons. I may not have got any outstanding marks but I got passes! It was marvellous at last to be able to enjoy working, to be intellectually stimulated. I realise now that before that everything had been far too easy for me. It didn't challenge me, I simply acquiesced in it.

That school was an experimental HAVO. I arrived as a supernumerary in form three and the great thing was that after form three you reached the optional subjects and could drop the languages. So at that moment everything in the garden was rosy and it looked as if I had conquered my difficulties.

Eventually, however, things went wrong, as just before the summer holidays the nice headmaster fell ill and then I was sent away from the school. The deputy head who then took over couldn't stand me. You see, I had a brother at the same school who was brainy, the only thing was he refused to work. I had three of his teachers and they all thought: oh no, here comes another one — when I'm completely the opposite!

So the day came when a letter arrived saying I had to leave. Well, as you might expect my mother blew her top; she thought I'd upset the apple-cart. But I said I wasn't aware I'd done anything wrong, I'd had no inkling of the black cloud hanging over me.

Eventually our doctor went into it — he was on the parents' committee — and he said: 'You can't be cross with her, as she hasn't done anything'. It was simply that they couldn't tolerate making an exception, with me as a supernumerary getting a report which meant that I would go up to the next class.

I was doing very well at that school. I grasped everything during the lessons and really didn't need my books. I still got fail marks for history because the language mistakes were counted in. But with teachers who didn't pay so much attention to those, things went very smoothly. That's why I've never really learnt to study, sitting crouched over books I mean. That's given me a great deal of trouble — and still does. Right up to this day I still don't know what it is to study. That's a result of my always having been below my proper level.

Meanwhile, having put up with all that squabbling at school, I was now 18. It was clear to everybody that I was out-growing the school. As a child I'd intended to be a doctor. I had to study medicine, and I would. So you can understand that when that option was blocked off, my whole world was shattered. It was a big blow to me.

I'M STILL BELOW MY PROPER LEVEL

I had to do something, of course, once I'd finished school. So with my tail between my legs I started on a course to be a beauty specialist. I failed it three times but eventually got the diploma. But I couldn't see myself setting to work doing that so I embarked on physiotherapy. I failed at that as well, of course, in the theory, and again the next year even worse than in the first year. Then my mother went along to talk to them and final-ly I was admitted to the second year as a supernumerary. But in that year there were more problems and I gave it up. At that moment I felt like the biggest failure in the world and went abroad.

There I landed up in the hotel trade. I blossomed, because I suddenly turned out to be able to do something. I was appreci-ated. That's very important, to be able to show off what is actu-ally in you. At school there is always one barrier after another to stop you being given your due — certainly if you're dyslex-ic. And a whole slice of your potential stays unexploited. But in the outside world you can make use of many more sides of your potential. And that's why adults with dyslexia do sometimes land on their feet after all.

Myself, I've never had that feeling. In every job I felt rest-less. Although I sometimes had a temporary victory, I would eventually get the idea that I didn't belong there, that I could do better, that I wasn't completely fulfilling myself.

That's why there came a day when I returned to Holland. I applied for masses of jobs, of course, but eventually I was taken on by a big multinational. I started off there in the internal ser-vices department of the industrial division. When I applied I told them honestly: I'm word-blind. The personnel manager asked: 'What is that? What does it imply?' And I told him how it meant that I couldn't write error-free sentences.

Of course, the language problem showed up once I was at work. I ignored it to the extent that I said: 'I told you so'. But it was included in my assessment each time. Each year I was confronted by it, until I could have wept. People didn't know what it was, it irritated them.

Then I had a boss who said: 'There's an end to it. We won't mention it any more'. He knew what he was talking about, as he had a dyslexic child himself. 'But', he said, 'I never realised that it could still be a problem when you're older'. Of course I'm seriously affected, whereas in the case of his child it had almost been overcome already.

I came much more into my own when he was my boss, which he was for two years, but people like that move on, they're birds of passage. I wanted to be off too. I had been there for three years and I am somebody who generally wants to be somewhere else after a year. You know why? If I'm below my proper level a time comes when I don't find it challenging any more. And I hate having to do my work like a stupid automaton. So I said to the company: 'I want to do a professional options test. Let's just see what it comes up with'. Well, I did it and of course I had to beg for the results. And what do you think they were? A position at an intermediate or higher level! So it was clear that I was in a sort of suspended animation and I wouldn't rest until I found myself in a suitable job.

When will society realise that it needs to recognise the worth of us dyslexics and get out of us what there is in there? Surely our talents can be put to good use? So at that professional options consultancy they said I would do outstandingly in computers. They said: 'You can do it but the training will take too long. And of course you will find the examinations a stumbling block'. They therefore advised against it. For the job I have now I needed the high school (HBS*) leaving certificate, but luckily they gave me a chance all the same. But they did impose the condition that I do an advertising training course. And I was perfectly prepared to do that except, of course, that I'd be running up against exams again. As I don't have a school-leaving certificate I wasn't allowed to do that course and therefore I first did the bridging course. I nearly got bogged down in that right at the start!

That exam was multiple choice — a disaster, I can tell you! But I went in advance to the lady who introduced it and said: 'I'm word-blind, I won't be able to cope with the time allowed for reading'. She was a bit taken aback, she'd heard alarm bells ringing. But she said: 'When you come to the exam just report to me then and I'll take it into account. And if the time is up and you haven't finished, let me know'. That was ideal, of course.

As far as the first part was concerned I did finish. My nerves were pretty frayed, of course. But not the second part. She then let me work on for 45 minutes. All the same I failed, because of my nerves. What happens is this: I read through the questions and know them all. Then I want to start writing and suddenly I no longer know anything. Absolutely nothing.

The fact that I've never learnt to study also plays a part. You read a book through and you know it. It's simply that you can't reproduce it. Then if you also take those reading problems into account, as a result of which you sit crouched over the text for an eternity looking for a connection, plus the time pressure, all those factors make you go off the boil and then you're just in a fog.

When I'd failed I went to the lady and we went through the exam together. I knew everything. She was very surprised, because it was not possible to deduce from my work that I had any real mastery of the subject. It was more a sort of wave motion: at first things would go well for a good stretch, then badly for a while, then well again, then at the end badly again. I went over it and she said: 'Do you know what, I'll put you right at the back. In a corner. And just ignore the time aspect'. I got there and it was organised to perfection. So I went and sat down and what do you think, the invigilators — they meant well, mind! — they came up to me saying: 'Everything all right? Getting on OK?' And that takes your concentration away. I worked on the first section for a quarter of an hour. The lady was surprised when I handed it in. I went twenty minutes over time on section two. They did leave me in peace for that. That was the marketing part. I passed it with a 7 but I failed the advertising section again. A 5. The first time I'd failed with two 5s, so the new marks were a bitter blow. Generally I fail with 1s and 2s and you accept that. But this was so close.

I was allowed to take the advertising section again orally. Not that that went all that smoothly either, mind. The lady literally had to draw everything out of me, I completely clammed up. But she said: 'I feel that you have mastered the material'. And ultimately she dragged me through.

That was a six-month course but I spent about two years on it. So now I have to do the course proper. I want to do it very much, 'but', I said at work, 'don't make it compulsory for me to do that exam, as it makes no sense at all to do that'.

When I came back to Holland ten years ago I naturally applied for I forget how many jobs and was just rejected. Because of my age, or because: 'You haven't got the qualifications for that'. This company was an exception, because they said: 'References are more important to us than certificates'. In my case they have to abide by that. I've always thought: 'You took me in, we'll see whether you're going to get rid of me now!'

ALWAYS KNOCKING

It's difficult, of course, to decide what in your adult life is to be put down to dyslexia and what is part of my personality and separate from dyslexia. There comes a time when you can't separate them any more. And if you accept that, what I can say is: I feel I must always be knocking, always showing what I can do, proving myself.

That's something I experience very strongly at work. I am single, so your work is a very important part of your life. I assume I'll be working until I'm 55 and I'm 38 now. That's why I've always said: 'I want to have a job that isn't a dead end. I want the potential to go further, as I refuse to sit on the same stool for evermore'. That test report does give a long list of suggestions, but doesn't indicate one single route. I can still go in any direction, but the middle rank where I am now is a disaster as far as getting ahead is concerned. I now work in the advertising department, so I'm always being confronted by my handicap. I'm often skilful in managing to camouflage it, incidentally, but people somehow feel that it's there. They try to get me for it or tick me off for it. We work with advertising agencies and when we're compiling leaflets and so on I get the wording read through by the person ultimately responsible for it, as I'm completely at sea.

Fortunately my task is a co-ordinating one, not a production one, so I can write little or badly. If something needs writing I'll do anything to get out of it. I don't even send Christmas cards, I prefer to do it by phone. What you do notice is that your handicap trains you terrifically. I program everything into my brain, in fact my memory is my files. That is an adaptation, just as deaf people learn to lip-read and blind people learn to rely on their hearing.

You mustn't come up with difficult words with me either. I can't pronounce them properly, so I'll always avoid them. I often just don't know what they mean. And if you've got something like that it becomes more and more noticeable as time goes by, until you can hardly talk normally any more. If you talk in basic language, though, people don't understand you. But the silly thing is that nine times out of ten the people themselves don't understand what they mean by more complicated words. They pick them up and throw them in everywhere. In our company 'flexible' is a vogue word, for instance. If you say 'adaptable' they get irritated or give you a funny look.

In my opinion dyslexia involves handicaps but also has some strong points. For instance I still can't tell right from left. I always have to look: oh yes, my watch is on my left wrist. It's a reason, I think, why I've turned letters round for a long time — the s's, p's, b's and d's and so on. And if I'm going to see people who explain the way to drive there I can follow it for a time but after that I think: chatter on as you please, it'll be all right.

I always keep a map in the car and if they give me the address I can find it OK. And even better is this: I can remember it the next time. Then I drive there just like that. It's no use you asking me the house number or even the name of the road, as I can't remember them. But I know exactly how to find the house. Even in the dark. And I can still find it again years later. Recently I went to see some friends I hadn't been to for fifteen years. And what do you think? I drive there without thinking. When I arrive I say: 'Now, you've had lots built on! This and that and so on and so forth'. Yet I always manage to drive so that I find the shortest route. I just feel where I need to go.

I can live perfectly well with the dyslexia. I accept it. It's not so much the dyslexia I'm fighting as society, which doesn't give us our due. Incidentally, I also think that battling against dyslexia, provided it's done properly, must make some sense, as what always strikes me is how one time it will be worse than another. It often goes up and down. Evidently a nervousness factor plays a part in it, which you ought to be able to switch off.

For me there remains the fact that I generally write words as I hear them. Certain letters I don't hear, and I omit those. Sound deafness, they call that. I also seem to have difficulty with the intonation. People point out to me that I put the stresses in the wrong place. But even if they say it a hundred times over I can't hear or see any difference. And then I think: what of it? Incidentally, I can remember music perfectly well.

As regards my languages I can't write a word of them but I can speak them. At school my French was the best of the three languages. At the moment the German has dropped away but I speak English just as if it were Dutch; after all I lived in England for seven years. But you mustn't ask me how to write it as then it would go completely wrong.

I dodge reading and writing at every opportunity. I haven't read a book yet this year. I read the papers fleetingly, and only ones where you only need to read the headlines! But OK, you stay abreast of what's happening by watching TV and listening to the radio.

The funny thing is that when I went to school I was keen to learn to read. And that's still in me somewhere even now, but I simply can't bring it out. I read out loud, in fact. Not really, but I formulate everything. So I just can't race through it like that. It goes word by word. And now and then you read a whole sentence again.

Now that I'm older it's more a question of having become myself, I think. When you're young you drift so, you're so dependent on people who happen to be in your life. A single nasty teacher, for example, can make or break you. It's almost impossible to overcome that. As far as I'm concerned I had a difficult school career, but I could have done worse. Every time, my mother came to the rescue and thought up solutions. She's been a tower of strength and I look on that as an excellent foundation.

Commentary by Specialists

DYSLEXIA IS NOT SOMETHING THAT PASSES

Dyslexia is not something that passes, even in adulthood. You continue to carry your specific weak and strong sides with you. However, the extent to which you have to confront them depends a little on the choices you make. Of course, you can't avoid your dyslexia altogether, in our culture which is in large measure based on the written word. But many adults cultivate a certain skill which enables them to keep to a minimum their need to face the implications of their reading and writing difficulties.

Firstly this can be done by choosing an occupation that has nothing to do with the two problem areas. And secondly, the possibilities of evading the difficulties in daily life are legion. Aids such as the telephone and television play a great part in this. In short, if they want to, a dyslexic person can 'duck out' once their schooldays are over and never have to disclose their dyslexia again. One suspects that in fact a large number of people do exactly that.

But it is not so simple for everyone. There are those who cannot reconcile themselves to the threat of their remaining deficient in certain aspects and who therefore apply themselves to those areas to a greater extent. When their schooldays are over they definitely want to master a foreign language. Or write children's books. Or become teachers. And that very wanting often turns out to be sufficient to enable them to achieve their goals. Via detours and sometimes dead ends dyslexic people ultimately arrive where they want to be. They will overcome enormous hurdles and master a great deal of knowledge, but: they are still dyslexic. This dyslexia is evidenced afresh in each new phase of their lives. One then has to adjust once more to the different circumstances. Fear of failure, of exams, insecurity, doubt — in new situations everything one thought one had conquered rears its ugly head once more, to be held under control for a while once more until the situation has stabilised.

Dyslexia does not go away, but it can be managed in accordance with one's own choices. Whereas at school one was totally dependent on the existing structure and the prevailing norms, in adulthood one can oneself give more form and content to what has come to be a major part of one's personality: dyslexia.

QUESTIONS

Do dyslexic people also have greater difficulty learning to speak foreign languages? Or is it only writing them that is a problem?

The best way for people with dyslexia to learn to speak a foreign language is to learn it in the country concerned. Problems only arise when the foreign language has to be read or written. For then the verbal–visual and visual–verbal connections are needed again, and these operate less well in dyslexic people. As long as a dyslexic person can stay with the visual aspect all will be well; as long as they remain within the auditory–verbal area things will go reasonably well; but if they have to switch backwards and forwards between the visual and verbal there will be trouble.

Nevertheless it is the case that in relation to learning a foreign language, reading and writing form important practice options, which will tend to inhibit dyslexic people rather than help them. As a result, learning foreign languages will probably be a slow business for them.

Is it possible, by means of 'part certificates' or something like that, for dyslexic people to meet the demand from society for diplomas at their own level?

Not in the UK. Examination certificates are seen to be either of a certain universal standard or not awarded. The use of aids, as already mentioned, or extra time, give the candidates an equal chance. Most examination results are graded and very few are now on a pass/fail basis.

Glossary

(The first occurrence in the text of the following items is indicated by an asterisk.)

Bridging class: After primary school, Dutch children go to the 'bridging class', which is the first year of secondary education, a kind of 'bridge' between primary and secondary school. After that year, the teachers advise about the level of education and type of school that the child is best suited for.

Cito test: A test given to children leaving primary school, to determine their academic level and to advise them which type of secondary school would suit them best.

Educational Advisory Service. See Schools Advisory Service.

HAVO: Senior general secondary education, following on from MAVO, with more subjects in the curriculum and higher standards.

HEAO: As for LEAO, but at a higher level, equivalent to HAVO.

HBS: The former name of a type of VWO school.

ITO: Technical education for normal children where the emphasis lies on the individual.

IVO: Individually oriented secondary education, at schools which have a special curriculum which allows pupils to study at their own rate, individually guided, but being prepared for the usual diplomas in secondary education. See also MAVO.

Jena-Plan school: A type of school designed after the ideas of the German educationalist, Peter Perterson, and named after the Dutchman, Jena, who developed the idea. This type of school is especially known for its vertical group character, where children of different ages can be in one group.

173

Junior Technical School: See LTS/LBO.

LEAO: Vocational education specialising in economics and administration, at the LAVO level, below both MAVO and HAVO.

LOM school: Primary school for children with learning disabilities. Referred to as 'Remedial School' in the text.

Lower Horticultural School: A school where children can receive education in the basics of gardening and horticulture.

LTS/LBO: Junior secondary technical/vocational school. The curriculum starts with language training (reading and writing) and other basic topics like arithmetic and geography and gradually introduces more technical subjects (e.g. building, motor mechanics, electrical engineering, catering, home economics, agricultural education, etc.), the final years being more vocationally oriented. The LTS or LBO gives pupils admission to senior secondary vocational education.

MAVO: Junior general secondary education, at schools with six or seven compulsory and optional subjects, Dutch and one modern foreign language being compulsory, leaving options from Frisian, history and civics, geography, biology, chemistry, physics, mathematics and economics. Sometimes expressive subjects like drawing, handicraft or music are added; some schools even offer Spanish, Russian, social studies or history of art.

MLK school: A primary school for the educationally subnormal.

MULO: Former name of a type of school between primary and secondary education, now superceded by the MAVO schools.

'Remedial School': See LOM school.

Rijksscholengemeenschap: State comprehensive school, composed of what might previously have been several separate schools (e.g. MAVO–HAVO or MAVO–HAVO–VWO). In the past, all schools were independent of each other, but following fairly recent national legislation, groups of schools have been made to cooperate and integrate in this way.

Schools Advisory Service (SAD/SBD): Advises schools about the curriculum and improvements to it, screening and diagnosis of children with special problems, etc. The nearest UK equivalent would be the Educational Psychology Service, or the Special Educational Needs Support Service.

'Supernumerary': A person who sits in on a course, not to prepare for formal exams but out of interest. (Dutch *Toehoorder* = 'Listener'.)

ULO: More or less the same as MULO, with a less extended curriculum.

VWO: Pre-university education, where subjects are taken on a somewhat higher level than at a HAVO school, and may include Greek or Latin.

ZMLK/ZMOK: Schools for children with extreme learning difficulties. In the UK the equivalent would be a school for children with emotional and behavioural difficulties (EBD schools).

Very few of these have British equivalents, but

LOM school: School for children with Moderate Learning Difficulties (MLD school).

MLK school: School for children with Severe Learning Difficulties (SLD school).

The UK now has a much more formalised system — Primary and Secondary schools. Primary schools are sometimes divided into Infants and Juniors with the transition in the summer after the 7th birthday. The transition from Primary to Secondary is in the summer after the 11th birthday in England and Wales, after the 12th in Scotland. Most Secondary schools are comprehensive although there are now a few City Technology Colleges — highly selective and extremely well resourced — in one or two urban areas. Children who cannot benefit from normal Primary or Secondary schools attend Special schools.